J.R.'s Cookbook

World Wrestling Entertainment™

J.R.'s Cookbook

True RINGSIDE Tales,

BBQ and *Down Home*

RECIPES

By Jim "J.R." Ross

with Jan Ross & Dennis Brent

POCKET BOOKS

New York   London   Toronto   Sydney   Singapore

This book is a publication of Pocket Books, a division of Simon & Schuster, Inc.,
under exclusive license from World Wrestling Entertainment, Inc. All rights reserved,
including the right to reproduce this book or portions thereof in any form whatsoever.
For information address Pocket Books, 1230 Avenue of the Americas, New York, NY 10020

ISBN: 0-7434-6504-0

Photos on pages v, xiv, 1, 4, 73, 105, 119, 123, 183, 194, 197,
201, 204, 216, 217, 236, 258, 265 (lower left), 271, 279
Courtesy of Jim Ross. Photos on pages 259, 260, 261, 264 (lower left),
265 (upper right), 274 (left) Dennis Bryant.
Insert photos by Amos Chan.

All other photos Copyright © 2003 World Wrestling
Entertainment, Inc. All Rights Reserved.

First Pocket Books printing June 2003

10 9 8 7 6 5 4 3 2 1

POCKET and colophon are registered trademarks of
Simon & Schuster, Inc.

For information regarding special discounts for bulk purchases,
please contact Simon & Schuster Special Sales at
1-800-456-6798 or business@simonandschuster.com

Design by Richard Oriolo

Visit us on the World Wide Web
http://simonsays.com/
http://www.wwe.com

PRINTED IN THE U.S.A.

This book is dedicated to my late mama,
Elizabeth Ann Sheffield Ross,
who always worked one or two jobs outside
our home, but never failed to provide our
family with delicious home
cooking every day.

Acknowledgments

Many people have been instrumental in making this project become a reality. My heartfelt thanks to the McMahon family for providing this opportunity and the many good folks in WWE, especially those in Creative Services and Marketing, including Stacey Pascarella and Donna Goldsmith, for their tireless efforts on behalf of this project. I would also like to thank Kevin Dunn and his hardworking crew at our television facility. My thanks to Margaret Clark, our editor at Pocket Books, for her patience and guidance. I also want to thank my friends and neighbors Dennis and Lynn Brent for all their efforts and their dedication to this labor of love. Finally, I want to thank my wonderful wife, Jan, who learned to cook from her two Italian grandmothers in Pittsburgh, whose legendary culinary skills are definitely "restaurant quality."

Introduction

I want to personally thank you, the reader, for checking out our newest cookbook. I am sure you are going to enjoy the recipes and the tales from the road of sports entertainment. Many of these recipes are tried-and-true country cookin' dishes that have been in my life ever since I can remember. We did not have too much growing up, but we always had great, homemade food, and enjoying it was a family affair. I will never forget those wonderful days or the aromas that poured out of my mama's tiny kitchen. Being a native Oklahoman, BBQ and grilling have been a right of passage for me since my daddy first taught me how to light a grill. I think you will enjoy these recipes too, and they will hopefully give you cause to spend more quality time with your family and friends. My tales from the road are a selection of stories from my twenty-five-plus years in the sports entertainment business, including many never-before-seen photos that I think you will also enjoy. The Ross family hopes that your family will enjoy this cookbook as much as we have enjoyed putting it together for you.

Thanks and happy eatin'!!

—Jim "J.R." Ross

Contents

OK, FOLKS, LET'S GET THIS SHOW STARTED . . .

First off, let's get right down to business. I've got to make it clear that *barbecuing* and grilling are two totally different things that are easily confused, but they are as different as night and day, kind of like a Cage match is not the same as a Texas Death match. Each type of outdoor cooking has its group of loyalists, and there's nothing wrong with that.

I love them both, but they are completely different animals. Southerners, where I come from, swear on the family Bible that barbecuing is better; they believe in slowly *smoking* pork and beef over a low fire until the meat falls off the bone. That all sounds great to me and *I love it!*

Folks up north and out west are partial to grilling and think that the meats should be seared over red-hot coals. And in today's modern world where time is everything, it seems that in general grilling has become more common, as it is faster and easier. People just don't have the time to devote to waiting maybe six to twelve hours for meats to properly smoke. Barbecuing is like a religion. The techniques and recipes have been passed down from generation to generation. I like them both, don't get me wrong, but I'm going to mostly focus on grilling, since that is what most people do now because of busy schedules.

When I am at home, I grill. When I'm on the road, especially down south, there's nothing I enjoy better than dropping in at a great BBQ joint and enjoying all those hours they put into smoking those ribs, pork, and beef. I could sit there all day letting those smoked meats melt in my mouth, savoring the taste that can come only from *many* hours smoking utilizing wood and low heat. Leave that to the experts and those that have the time. Otherwise, I'd suggest grilling.

Regardless of what you prefer, when it comes to making a quick and easy family dinner, there is one thing that everyone seems to agree with: grilling is good and makes almost anything taste better. And it is faster. With proper seasoning, marinades, and sauces, you can create some fantastic meals that are easy to fix for yourself or for the whole family in a short time and people will rave what a great "barbecue'er" you are. Oh well, you can't educate the whole world.

grilling is so **good**
you can't sit still
and **eat** it

GRILL THESE NUMBERS!!

Americans in 2001 held 3.1 *BILLION* cookouts around this great land of ours, which is *up* from 2.7 *BILLION* in 1995, according to Mediamark Research, Inc. Average folks like you, me, and our neighbors **grill** an average of 4.6 times per month, in season, which is considered by most to be Memorial Day through Labor Day or May through September.

Around the J.R. house, we grill the year 'round probably, an average of five to six times per month even in the winter! Research shows that 57 percent of backyard grillers use their grills ***year-round,*** too. Now that's what I'm talking about! Over 15 million BBQ-grill units are sold every year in the USA alone, which is a mind-boggling number in my view. In the United States, 32 percent of BBQ'ers live in the South, 23 percent in the West, 26 percent in the Midwest, and 19 percent in the Northeast.

Everybody has their own reasons for grilling and BBQing, but recent research shows that the primary reasons, in order, are as follows:

1. **Like the flavor**

2. **It's easy**

3. **Enjoy entertaining guests**

4. **Enjoy being outdoors**

5. **Like the casual atmosphere**

6. **Like to avoid heating up the house**

7. **People find it personally satisfying**

Grilling is not simply a southern redneck thing, as some perceive. It has about as much mass appeal as anything you can think of, and, boy howdy, do the groceries taste good on the grill! And they are healthy, too!

. . . boy howdy, do the groceries **taste** good on the grill!

J.R.'S LIST OF EIGHT REQUIRED UTENSILS FOR PROPER GRILLING

Spatulas Metal, not plastic! Long-handled spatulas are best so you don't burn your wrist. Keep several handy so you can use a different one for your chicken or fish and a different one for your hamburger patties or turkey burgers.

Tongs Spring-loaded is best. These also come in long-handled versions. You can use these instead of your fingers to turn meat over, move vegetables around, all kinds of things. They are a must.

Basting Brushes You can use brushes specifically made for this or you can use a two-to-three-inch-wide paintbrush you buy at the hardware store. It certainly doesn't have to be fancy, but use a new clean one, not one you painted the garage with last week! These are good for painting the sauce on the meats while they are on the grill. Also, I like natural bristles, not plastic ones. Some folks use cotton "mops" for basting their ribs and meats. That's totally fine with me. Just get that good sauce all over those baby-backs!

Wire Grid or Hinged Wire Basket These can be found at your local home improvement center. They are cheap and are great for grilling items that might normally fall through your grill, like shrimp, scallops, or vegetables. The hinged wire basket is also great for fish and other delicate food that might break apart when turning. You can turn all the filets over at the same time very easily!

Wire Brush This is a must for cleaning your grill when you are done. Put some elbow grease behind it and give it a good scrubbing while it's still hot. You can get a nice long-handled wire brush for cleaning grills just about anywhere. It works much better than a steel wool pad and keeps your hands cleaner too.

Skewers These are indispensable for making kebobs. You can get them made of metal or wood. With metal skewers, the food sometimes turns or slips around while you are trying to rotate them on the grill and not everything turns at the same time, so get the kind that has a spiral around it, versus straight square edges. It sometimes works better for turning the food. I prefer the wood skewers for nonslipping, but soak them in water for thirty to sixty minutes first to keep them from burning.

Drip Pan A drip pan is used to collect and trap the juices that drip off the cooking meat, either to keep the fire from flaming up, or to make gravy with later on. The pan is placed between the heat source and the grill grate. Some people put some water in it to create steam. There are all kinds of commercial drip pans you can buy at the store, which is probably best, or in a pinch you can make one out of several layers of aluminum foil by turning up the edges.

Meat Thermometer This is an important yet inexpensive tool to use to make sure that your food is cooked to a certain temperature on the inside. In the case of beef a meat thermometer can help assure that you've reached a certain degree of "doneness," and with other foods, like poultry, to make sure it is cooked hot enough to kill any bacteria. If you just look at the outside of a piece of meat you cannot make an accurate judgment about the meat being "done." It is very easy to dry food out by waiting for it to "look right" or to keep slicing the food to look in it. Buy a meat thermometer at the store with a metal probe—it will make your grilling and cooking a lot easier, safer, and more consistent!

J.R.'S TIP—*On using forks to turn food—just so you know, I don't use these very much, if at all. The more you poke your food, the more juice it loses and the drier it gets. Anything you'd use a fork for, I'd rather see you use a tong or a spatula. Just grab that sucker and turn it over. You don't need to stab it to death, it's already dead.*

THESE ARE THE RULES FOR THE MAIN EVENT . . .

To do the best job you can, there are certain things you must do, or know, to make the food as tasty as possible. Here are some tips:

Know how hot the food is inside! Get a meat thermometer and know the internal temperature of the food that you are cooking. Not all grills cook food at the same rate, and there are many variables, including how hot the fire is. One constant is the temperature *inside* the food. There are all kinds of meat thermometers, from simple to fancy, but they all do the same thing. It will help make your food consistently good.

Know the temperature you are cooking at! All grills are different, plus there are variables including wind, how many times you open the lid and look at the food . . . Many grills include a built-in thermometer. If not, you can get an add-on thermometer pretty inexpensively at your local home improvement center. This is very helpful in making sure the temperature is hot enough to cook the meat all the way through.

Always use the cleanest fire you can to produce the best taste! Don't use charcoal starter if you can help it. Use one of those chimney-type charcoal starters. They are fast and efficient without using bad-tasting fluids. If you do use fluids, wait about forty-five minutes to allow the charcoal to burn down and to remove the taste of the petroleum distillates. That taste is never a good thing! If using wood, wait until it has been reduced down to coals before putting the food on. If using propane, clean out food ashes and debris occasionally from the pit and turn over and rotate the briquettes occasionally. Keep your grate clean by wire-brushing it after each use. Also, it is easier to wire-brush a hot grill than a cold one.

Don't overcook the food, thinking it will make the food "fall off the bone"! Anytime you overcook meat, it will dry it to the bone, but that has nothing to do with being tender.

Cleanliness is mandatory for good taste and good health! Always wash your hands before and after handling uncooked meats. Use paper towels, not the same cloth towels, to dry your hands. Keep your chicken on a separate plate from your beef, etc. Use different cooking utensils for the chicken, fish, and pork. Be aware that bacteria are everywhere and one of the purposes of cooking the food is to kill the bacteria. Be aware that cross contamination is very easy if you are not careful.

Your grill grates MUST BE HOT! Especially if you are grilling, as opposed to barbecuing. Have your fire at maximum temperature for at least twenty minutes before putting the food on. That way you get that ear-pleasing sizzle when you add the food, plus it makes those pretty grill marks that people look for on grilled food. It will also help keep the food from sticking when you turn it over. If your food is sticking to the grill, then it is *not* ready to be turned over! Easy tip, huh? When the meat releases easily or with a slight pull, it is ready to be turned. This tip *only* applies if your grill is hot, however.

"J.R., How Did You Get in This Business?"

Many people ask me how I got started in the sports entertainment business. I was fresh out of Westville, Oklahoma, high school—home of the Yellow Jackets—and was attending Northeastern State University in Tahlequah, Oklahoma, which is known for being the Cherokee Indian capital of the world.

In 1972, our fraternity Phi Lambda Chi, an animal house–like group of beer-drinking misfits, needed a fund-raiser for charity to improve our rather tarnished hell-raising image. Several of my "brothers" were also lifelong wrestling fans, and we decided to promote a wrestling match using promoter LeRoy McGuirk's stable of Cowboy Bill Watts and Danny Hodge–led talent, wrestlers we had seen on television.

My friend Jerry Donley and I drove to Tulsa where Championship Wrestling was headquartered, and met with Mr. McGuirk and the Big Cowboy to pitch our idea, and hopefully close the deal. I was passionate in my presentation, and we closed the deal and scheduled our date. I was told later in my career by LeRoy and Cowboy that they were impressed with my passion. I guess they were pleased with the pitch, because they hired me about a year and a half later and my journey in our wonderful business began.

Oh, by the way, the main event that night was Danny Hodge versus Skandor Akbar and it sold out Redman Field House.

SAVE YOUR RUMP!
Use a Meat Thermometer!

People are grilling out more and more. But there is more to outdoor barbecuing than just putting burgers on the grill!

Grillers need to think about food safety, and one way to ensure that is by using a food thermometer. Using a food thermometer is the only way to tell if food has reached a high enough temperature to destroy bacteria. Also, a food ther-mometer is the only reliable way to determine the "doneness" of meat, poultry, and fish. To be safe, these foods must be cooked to an internal temperature high enough to destroy any harmful microorganisms that may reside in the food.

"Doneness" refers to when a food is cooked to what the eye "thinks" is done, based on texture, appearance, and juiciness. Unlike the temperatures required for food safety, these are subject to personal preference.

But recent research has shown that color and texture indicators may not be reliable, and that is why food thermometers are a good tool to have handy when grilling.

There is a difference between safety and "doneness." For example, a roast or steak that is not pierced in any way during processing or preparation and reaches an internal temperature of 145° F is safe to eat.

According to the USDA, most food-borne bacteria are destroyed at temperatures between 140° and 160° F, but for best quality, meat and poultry require various temperatures for "doneness."

These include:

Hamburgers	**160° F**
Ground poultry	**165° F**
Medium-rare steaks	**145° F**
Well-done steaks	**170° F**
Poultry breast	**170° F**
Poultry dark meat	**180° F**

A backyard chef looking for a visual sign of "doneness" might continue cooking until the steak is overcooked and dry, but a smart griller that reads J.R.'s book is using a meat thermometer to check for temperature "doneness" and can feel assured that the food has reached a safe temperature and is not undercooked.

Most thermometers will give an accurate reading within two to four degrees Fahrenheit, but the reading will only be correct if the thermometer is placed in the proper location in the food. Stick the probe to the center of the thickest part of the meat. C'mon, J.R. doesn't want his fans to get sick!

food thermometers are a **good tool** to *have handy when grilling*

THE X FACTOR OF THE BLACK HAT

My trademark black hat has become a fixture of my TV character's persona every week on WWE *Raw,* but it did not come easily. Good ol' J.R. wearing a cowboy hat on television was not my idea. It was the brainchild of the chairman of the company, Vince McMahon, who thought, with my Oklahoma drawl, that I should look more like I sounded and the cowboy hat would be a perfect fit. My resistance to this "gimmick" was basically a by-product of my own ego. I had never worn a hat even as a kid or young man growing up in a state where cowboy hats were as commonplace as pickup trucks and country music. I felt like my television persona had been established long before I came to WWE in 1993, and it did not need any changing. Or so I thought. Some of my business associates, sensing my displeasure with this idea, ribbed me unmercifully that not only was I going to be wearing a hat, but a **"Porter Wagoner"**–style glittery western jacket, cowboy boots, and perhaps even chaps, for goodness' sakes. I would be ready for the Grand Ole Opry! I stupidly bought into the rib and allowed my stubbornness to take over. And then I got to thinking . . . First, I figured out the rib and saw it for what it was . . . some folks' lame attempt to assist me out the door for their own perverse, personal gain. Second, I realized I had become what I totally despised in this business, an egomaniacal veteran who resisted change for the betterment of the product. So I began proudly wearing a cowboy hat on TV and I have never looked back. As a matter of fact, I think it has been great for my career. Cowboy hats are a part of true Americana.

My brand of choice is a Resistol hat made in Garland, Texas, USA. I own probably half a dozen or so black felt hats and have, over the years, donated many of them to charities, often with the Make-A-Wish Foundation to auction off for their fund-raising efforts. My most prized hat is the one I wear most every week on *Raw* and all PPVs and it's a top-of-the-line 200X Resistol, given to me one year at Christmas by **Stone Cold Steve Austin.** Within the hat-making community, the more *X*s a hat has, the better quality it is. Pure beaver fur hats are usually 10X or 20X, so you can see that my 200X hat is at the top of the line and sells for a pretty penny. To me, my favorite hat is priceless, and it will be on my head for as long as I have the privilege of broadcasting for WWE.

TOP TEN "J.R." CLICHÉ'S

10 "He better cover those words in **BBQ** sauce because he's going to have to eat them!"

9 "Hell, fire and brimstone."
Always seemed like it fit Kane's entrance and his persona.

8 "Restaurant quality." Anything uniquely good. "He just got a restaurant-quality butt whipping!"

7 "Jezebel." Has been around forever with its origins in the "Good Book." It's an apt way to describe an evil woman.

6 "Business is about to pick up!" I normally use this one when things are looking up for the hero.

5 "Bowling shoe ugly." Sometimes when a situation, sometimes not by design, gets real ugly . . . bowling shoe ugly!

4 "Goofy as a pet coon." From personal experience, I can tell you domesticated coons go a little goofy and *do not* make good pets.

3 "Government mule." In the 1800s along with land, our government oftentimes awarded families with mules to help farm their new land. These animals were often, unfortunately, beaten and abused.

& CATCHPHRASES

2 "Limbertail." I was umpiring a college baseball game many years ago and the pitcher could not or would not throw strikes. His coach, the brother of former OU (Oklahoma University) football great and Texas coach Darrell Royal, gave the kid the hook. As the player headed to the bench Coach Royal turned to me and said, "Looks like my little pitcher got a case of the Limbertail," which meant he lost his courage.

1 And the number one J.R. catchphrase is . . . "SLOBBERKNOCKER." An age-old football term I first heard when I was in elementary school. It describes pronounced physicality with hard hitting, hard enough to induce "slobber" from one's mouth.

Just another high-spirited announcers meeting. The King and I are attempting to convince Tazz that *Raw* is superior to *SmackDown!*

BASIC GRILLING TIMES

Grilling is all a matter of time. You don't want to dry out the food, but you do want it cooked enough to be *healthy.* If you just slap food on the grill and "eyeball" it, judging when it's done by looks, chances are it will not be done enough or it will be overcooked. Here are some *tips* to getting the food cooked just right. These times are for cooking the food medium well. Turkey burgers and chicken should be thoroughly cooked.

HAMBURGER PATTIES

1-inch thick	5 minutes per side. Add a minute per side for medium-well done and two minutes more on each side for well done (or charcoal'ed, as a friend of mine likes to say).

TURKEY BURGERS

1-inch thick	6 minutes per side

PORK CHOPS

1-inch thick	14–18 minutes per side
½-inch thick	6–8 minutes per side

FISH (FILET OR STEAK)

1-inch thick	5–6 minutes per side
½-inch thick	3–5 minutes per side
1-inch thick	2–2½ minutes per side

STEAK

2-inch thick	10–12 minutes per side
1-inch thick	7–8 minutes per side
½-inch thick	5–6 minutes per side

CHICKEN BREASTS

	5–7 minutes per side

FACTOIDS FROM J.R.'S COOKBOOK FILE

Perfect Meal for J.R. Grilled rib eye, fried potatoes with purple onions, grilled asparagus or fresh steamed broccoli, BBQ beans, Texas toast, and iced sun tea with fresh lime with my Granny's Apple Dumplings for dessert.

NUMBER ONE CONTENDER: Slow-smoked baby back ribs, BBQ beans with chopped purple onions, a baked potato with BBQ sauce lightly poured on top, and homemade coleslaw with homemade huckleberry cobbler for dessert.

Simple Meal . . . or Snack, If You Will! Crock-Pot–prepared pinto beans, homemade corn bread, a slice of purple onion with a little ketchup for seasoning all mixed together in a LARGE bowl. Very simple, very good, and even better on day two!

NUMBER ONE CONTENDER: Apple butter with peanut butter sandwich on Martin's potato bread and a cold glass of 2% milk. Okay . . . maybe TWO sandwiches!

I wish I knew how to cook Chinese food because I really like it and so many dishes are very healthy, especially the spicy chicken dishes. It's just easier to have it delivered by the "experts."

Why Do I Like Grilling? It's usually done outside at a relaxed pace, and unless I'm not paying attention, it usually ends up with good results, which puts a smile on the face of family and friends. The feeling of accomplishment and doing something well for others is very rewarding, plus it reminds me of simpler times in my life when things were slower paced and more appreciated. Grilling, to me, is very therapeutic. And it's cheaper than seeing a shrink.

How Did You Come Up with Your BBQ Sauce Recipe? I vividly remember my late mama making BBQ sauce on our stove in our little four-room house that I grew up in as a kid in rural Oklahoma. The entire house smelled so great! After traveling around the world for years in the wrestling business and sampling BBQ sauce in a variety of states and establishments, I pretty much knew what I really liked and what I did not. We wanted to develop a sauce that I liked, and that I thought others would too. We have done that after literally hundreds of hours of experimenting, with my wife leading the way in our kitchen at home. Our sauce is a labor of love, a tribute to my late mama, ol' JR's vision, and my wife's recipe filled with love and passion.

My wife, Jan, she's the pretty lady on the right, is the brains behind J.R.'s BBQ Sauce and many of the recipes in this cookbook.

My Favorite BBQ Places to Eat These are the nonfranchised establishments that are family owned and operated. These families are committed to producing a product that *their* family is proud of, and they serve it with pride and love of their product. Places like Fat Matt's Rib Shack in Atlanta, Earl's in Oklahoma City, and Arthur Bryant's in Kansas City serve every meal to their customers just as if their customers were family.

Beef or Pork?? Pork, the "other" white meat, is hard to beat on the BBQ, especially the baby back ribs! But a slow-cooked, juicy brisket or a great steak is hard to beat too. I guess I am an equal opportunity eater when it comes to beef and pork. I suppose you could compare it to watching an Oklahoma Sooners football game at home in Norman, Oklahoma, or on the road.

Propane or Charcoal? For convenience and the time factor, it has to be propane. When time is not a factor and a day has been set aside for cooking, however, charcoal is hard to beat for true flavor, especially when seasoned wood chips are also used.

Favorite Seasonings? That's like asking who is my favorite all-time wrestler. There are almost too many to choose. Certainly on the list would be seasoned salt and seasoned pepper, liquid smoke of most any flavor, a little cayenne pepper, and a touch of garlic powder. For grilled salmon I like to use honey and a little cinnamon sugar along with fresh squeezed lemon and lime. Favorite seasonings really depend on what I am cooking, my mood, and the time involved, because I have found that the longer you can season your food and let it set the better it usually tastes. Grilling should not be a "wham-bam, thank-you ma'am"–type proposition.

J.R.'S TOP TEN SURE SIGNS TO TELL IF

10 No problem using an airport named for a great man, Will Rogers, who died in an airplane crash.

9 Makes daily use of the term *fixin'*.

8 Received an excused absence from school to haul hay.

7 Knows that calf fries are really called mountain oysters.

6 The big shade tree in your front yard is really your carport and favorite parking place.

5 Your "condo at the beach" is actually a camping trailer at the lake.

4 On a regular basis you drive out of state to buy beer.

SOMEONE IS FROM OKLAHOMA

3 You planned your wedding around the O.U. football schedule.

2 Only your mama calls you by your full name, and then only when she's angry.

1 Named at least one son Bud, Barry, or Bob after one of the great Oklahoma football coaches.

THE TRIPLE THREAT!

How to Grill and Cook Some Great, "Restaurant-Quality" Steaks, Chicken, and Ribs

Grilling Steaks—
A Main Event in My Book

It is not difficult to grill a perfect steak. Timing is everything, as well as proper preparation. *Grilling* a steak is an easy meal for yourself or the whole family, and unless you don't eat red meat, this is as good as it gets! It's easy, and cooking time is only about twenty minutes. Time well spent, in my opinion.

Getting Down to Business . . .

Take the steak out of the refrigerator and let the meat reach room temperature. If it is in the freezer, put it in the refrigerator to defrost first, don't microwave it!

Trim off any excess fat. It will only cause your grill to flare up and make a mess in the fire pit. Strips of fat around the steak should not be more than a quarter-inch thick.

Rinse the steak under clean running water. Then wash and dry your hands.

Season the steak to your liking. Add some fresh cracked pepper, garlic powder, whatever you like. Don't put salt on the steak until after it is cooked, as the salt will dry out the meat. Some like to marinate the steak or baste it with sauce first. That's a personal choice.

Preheat your grill at high heat for at least ten minutes. If using coals, make sure you have a nice layer of white coals. If using gas then set it at a nice flame, but not too high once the preheating is done.

Oil the grate using a brush.

Place your steak on the grill and close the lid for one minute.

Lift the lid and turn the steak over. Close the lid and continue grilling for another minute.

Turn again and continue for 2 minutes.

Turn it over for the fourth time and continue grilling for 2 minutes.

Use a meat thermometer to check for doneness: 140° for rare, 150° for medium rare, 160° for medium, 165° for medium well, burnt for well done.

Remove from the grill and let the steak rest for 2 to 3 minutes before serving.

Letting the steak rest before you eat it is an important trick. This allows the juices to seep throughout the meat and gives you a much more flavorful steak.

J.R.'S TIP—*I've heard over and over from all kinds of "experts" that you're only supposed to turn a good steak once. In my opinion, whatever that is worth, this is not a good thing to do. Why? If you put your steak on and leave it for a few minutes waiting for one side to be all done, you'll notice that all the juice has risen to the top and is sitting there. Then when you flip it over, all of that good juice gets dumped on the coals and it's gone. I like to turn the steak over several times every few minutes and keep that good juice inside the meat. And that's all I've got to say about that. If any of those "experts" out there want to grill me on this, they know where to find me.*

Smooching a Billionaire's Butt on Live TV . . . and *Almost* Liking It.

The night I kissed Vince McMahon's butt on *Raw* has turned out to be one of the most controversial segments of television I've ever been a part of.

Originally I was not overwhelmed with the creative concept of the segment. I was most unhappy that I was not consulted or at least given a heads-up before it was discussed in the production meeting, which I did not attend, as I was doing promotional work for the event that night. I knew something was up when many of the staff and talent would not look me in the eye when I arrived at the building in Oklahoma City. That was very unusual, as we normally always joke around and enjoy casual conversation during downtime. That afternoon those conversations were unusually short. I thought I had bad breath or something!

Both of my daughters, their friends, and many of my childhood pals came to the event, which was a concern to me, but not a major one. It certainly wasn't a deal breaker for me. They have all been following my career obviously forever and knew that we often do some crazy stuff in our attempts to entertain our audiences and tell

a story. Some staff members thought it was pretty funny, the fact that I was going to be "humiliated" in front of my friends and family in my home state, but those that really know me know I always try to be a trouper and will do what is needed. It can be argued that the kissing-Vince's-butt segment was not the appropriate creative vehicle to make Mr. McMahon more of a villain, but the bottom line is that it worked. Perhaps more importantly we were attempting to make Undertaker a villain too, and by him assaulting "Good ol' J.R." in Oklahoma, it would elicit the appropriate response from the live crowd for our television viewing audience to experience and feel. My fellow Oklahomans did not like it one bit, and it came across on the TV screen. The genuine anger from the live audience transmitted well at home. Fans were incensed that I had to perform this degrading and humiliating stunt.

Mr. McMahon's overbearing antagonist persona is easy for him to do, as he is an easy villain to dislike, and the Oklahoma City crowd did not like him at all that night. Not one bit. He might as well have given them the "Hook 'em Horns" sign that night in Oklahoma.

Undertaker, on the other hand, may have been a failed experiment, because unlike Vince, Undertaker is harder to hate because of his decade-plus of in-the-ring dedication and hard work, which the majority of our fans respect and appreciate. Both Vince McMahon and Undertaker have been important people in my career, and they were going to get my best effort no matter what I thought of the creative concept.

However, at the time we did not know if we could take the popular big "Deadman" to the other side, so to speak, but it was certainly worth the attempt and the effort. There was never any doubt that I wouldn't do this segment, even if I totally despised it. This is really a team game, more than most people think. As the head of talent relations, I would set a bad example for others to follow if I cried like a spoiled baby and wanted things changed to better soothe my out-of-control ego. Unfortunately, I have seen this done too many times, and there was no way I was going to play that pathetic game. Wrestlers who are not as talented a performer as they would like the world and their peers to believe have oftentimes gone to those in charge—here it is Vince—to get something changed in a match, etc., so the talent doesn't "look bad" in their insecure mind. These talents are usually of the overpaid, veteran variety that should be either retired or asked to wear a diaper when reporting to work. Veteran stars oftentimes are without a doubt the most insecure participants in the entire genre. Talent should always be prepared to contribute to the creative side, and the decision makers should always listen to their suggestions and use them if they do not compromise the overall intent of the creative concept. But some talent cry like a pig stuck under a gate if they have to do something like *lose* a match, for God's sake, or pray tell be asked to elevate a young talent to the next level. I was *not* going to play that game, but I simply would have liked the respect to have been informed of what the creative department had in mind beforehand, and I did not get that on that particular day.

Would Vince really ask me or any of his staff to do a degrading stunt like that in the office? Of course not, but this is WWE television, where crazy stuff happens. It created a great bit of talk and moved a story line along. It all adds to the bottom line, which is entertaining our fans. It was one day out of 365 days in a year, and I got over it by breakfast.

One thing for sure—Mr. McMahon had an extremely clean-smelling backside that night. I'm not sure, but I think he's partial to baby powder, and 'Taker delivers one of the best punches in the business. At the end of the day, we pulled it off to the best of our ability and accomplished what creative wanted. My buddies still kid me about being an "ass-kisser," and I am sure my ex wives enjoyed the segment, if they saw it. Hey, maybe that's where creative got the idea!

Don't Chicken Out Now!
Grill That Chicken Right and Make It a Superstar!

As always, start with a clean grill grate. Hopefully you wire brushed it after the last time you used it. Rinse your chicken under running water and put it on a plate by itself. Then wash and dry your hands on a paper towel and throw the towel away. Don't put it back on the counter, but toss that sucker right in the trash. Raw chicken can be a source of all kinds of bacteria, otherwise known as "invisible foreign objects," something that is never a good thing. Don't let the raw chicken touch *anything* in your kitchen.

When grilling chicken, the main thing you have to do is to keep the chicken moist while cooking. There is nothing worse than dried-out chicken, no matter how much BBQ sauce you slap on it afterward. Dry as shoe leather does not make good eating in J.R.'s neck of the woods.

There are a few ways to keep your chicken moist when grilling. My favorite method to grill chicken and keep it moist is to marinate the chicken. You can use either a commercial brand or one of your own creation. The grocery store sells all types of marinades, both bottled and in mix form, so whatever you like, they probably have it. An easy one that is always good is Italian vinaigrette. Most people have a bottle of that in the fridge. Whatever you use, prepare your marinade and let the chicken soak in the liquid for at least a half hour in the refrigerator. The longer the better, no time limit. You can start it in the morning and let it marinate in the refrigerator until you are ready to start grilling when you get home, or you can even start it the night before. Poke the chicken with a fork in a few places while it is marinating so the flavors and moisture can be absorbed into the chicken.

Or you can force-feed your marinade into the chicken. A national steak chain has always had terrific grilled chicken breasts that I've always enjoyed. I was talking to someone who worked there once and asked what was their secret. When he told me, it made so much sense I had to try it! They marinate their chicken breasts in orange juice and 7UP! The carbonation bubbles force the sweetness of the orange juice into the chicken, and it really tastes great!

If you prefer not to marinate and would rather use BBQ sauce, don't put the sauce on too early in the cooking process, as the sugar in the sauce will caramelize and burn the chicken. Let the chicken cook for at least a minute on each side before brushing on the sauce. Once you slap that sauce on, keep basting the chicken until it is done. If you are cooking a chicken that still has the skin on it, the skin should be browned and very tasty after the sauce caramelizes.

When grilling chicken on a gas grill, keep the flame low. If you are using a charcoal grill, make sure that the chicken is not right on top of the coals. Raise the grate a bit higher than you would for a steak. Turn the chicken over often and keep those juices inside! If you walk away and do something else or get distracted, it will burn or dry out.

Later I will give you my wife's recipe for cooking a perfect whole bird in the oven, and it will be so moist, it'll fall right off the bone and melt in your mouth, I guarantee!

This Is Not a Rib! Serious Rib Information That All Outdoor Cookers Need to Know!

It is a simple fact that with all the great foods that people put in their smokers or on their grills, we cook more ribs than any other meat, other than hamburgers and hot dogs. Why is that? There is nothing in the outdoor cooking world that is more tasty than properly prepared ribs. People just love BBQ ribs, no doubt about it. Fabulous ribs become the stuff of legend. Good grill chefs guard their recipes as though they were front-row tickets to next year's *WrestleMania*. The "secrets" get passed down from generation to generation and sometimes are never even written down. Just talking about good ribs being served makes people sweat with anticipation.

Types of Ribs

First of all understand that when most folks talk about ribs they mean *pork* ribs. They do cook some fantastically delicious beef ribs down in Texas, but I suspect that most backyard grillers go for pork, and that's what we'll be talking about first. When you

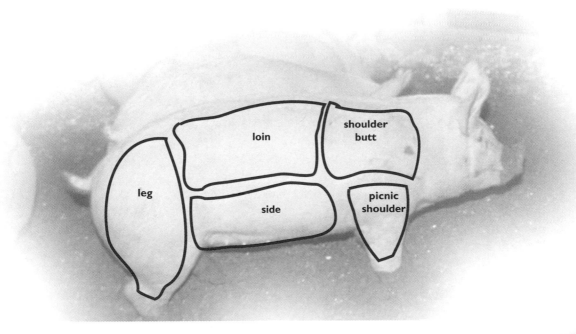

go to the market, you'll almost always find one of the following types of pork ribs and sometimes all three. You've got your spare ribs; baby back ribs; and country-style ribs.

Spare ribs are the traditional slab of ribs. They come from the belly of the pig along the side and behind the shoulder. There are usually eleven to thirteen long bones' worth. There is a layer of meat on top of the bones and between them, and they are the least expensive type of ribs, not that there's anything wrong with that! There are St. Louis–style ribs and Kansas City–style ribs. These are variations on spare ribs and refer to the way the ribs are cut and trimmed. Regardless of the way spare ribs have been trimmed for sale at the market, they all cook the same way and are great eating.

Baby back ribs used to be called loin ribs, but the term "baby back" sounds fancier, thanks to mass marketing and advertising by numerous restaurant chains. They are cut from the loin portion of the pig, the upper side of the ribs. There is a layer of meat over the bones and between them. They are shorter, smaller, leaner, and usually a lot more expensive than spare ribs. It's all good eating either way you go.

Country-style ribs are actually not ribs at all but are cut from right behind the upper portion of the shoulder and before the baby back ribs start. They are more like fatty pork chops than ribs. While they have more fat than any of the other types of ribs, the fat is in layers and the meat in between the layers is leaner and less mar-

This broadcast assignment of a Hog-Pen match reminded me of my Future Farmer of America days.

bled than most other ribs. They also have more good meat than the other types of ribs. A lot of folks don't know that, but these are great too, if you don't mind working through the fat.

What Type of Rib Is Best for Grilling and Barbecuing (Smoking)?

That depends, so let's go over some of the differences. Spare ribs are by far the most economical, and they are the best for smoking. They have a higher percentage of fat than baby backs, which explains the difference in cost. The higher fat content makes them less desirable to those unacquainted with the thrill of barbecuing or smoking, which makes them perfect for cooking low and slow. Barbecuing over low heat will melt the fat while keeping the ribs moist and juicy.

Baby backs have the advantage of having fantastic flavor and less fat, and this makes the baby back ribs more suited for grilling. They cook faster and don't require long, slow cooking times because there is not much fat. That's why most restaurants serve baby back ribs. They cook quicker, so the restaurant can serve the customer faster. Spare ribs can be grilled if you don't rush them, and smoked baby backs melt in your mouth. So keep in mind there are no hard-and-fast rules when it comes to cooking ribs, other than the more fat, the slower and longer you should cook them.

A lot of grillers don't mess with country-style ribs because they have much more fat than pork chops. Try them and grill them like pork chops. You might like them better than the leaner pork chops, because the chops can easily be overcooked, making them dry and tough. The country-style ribs will be a lot juicier, and the meat is fantastic.

Preparing Your Ribs

Pick a slab that is nice and thick, and has a little marbling of fat on the meat side. You'll still need to do a bit of trimming. Be sure to remove any additional hunks of fat that the butcher missed, leaving the natural

Not many "talkers" are brave enough to wear bib overalls with a tuxedo. That's pig slop on my jacket.

fat located "between the ribs." What we are looking for here is to remove the big pieces that lie on the outside of the meat. Now the ribs are ready for seasoning. Wars have been started over the proper method of seasoning ribs, and certain sections of the country will fight one another over a certain way to do it. Basically you can mop them with sauce or you can apply a "dry rub" of special seasoning. I won't get in the middle on this one, folks. I've had both, and *both* are mouth-watering good.

My favorite place for pork ribs is a small rib joint in Atlanta called Fat Matt's Rib Shack. It is a local legend in a semi-run-down neighborhood that has cars lined up all the way down the street waiting for a place to park. I'll have a rib sandwich now, and maybe one to take home for later! What's a rib sandwich? They serve you your grilled, smoked ribs with two slices of white bread on the side. You pull the meat off the bone and make your own sandwich and put some sauce on it. Easy to eat, and *man* is it good! It may not sound like restaurant fare to you, but the place has been open for many, many years, and the elite of Atlanta have all been spotted there. Teddy Long took Dennis Brent there one day, and Dennis brought me. Since then that wonderful taste has been etched in my brain. I'm happy to say they have my picture on their wall, along with years' worth of Blues legends that go there late at night.

When you are in the Lone Star state, ribs take on a whole new meaning! In Texas, *barbecue* means beef, not pork, and great beef ribs are a favorite of mine. Some people claim beef ribs are tough and fatty when barbecued. If your beef ribs are coming out tough, then you aren't cooking them long enough. Beef ribs need to be cooked at a low temperature for a long enough time to render the fat and tenderize the meat. Keep the smoker at around 200–225° F and cook them for about 8 to 10 hours, and they will melt in your mouth and not be all fatty or greasy. Oh, they are *so* good, like eating filet mignon on a stick! A place in Atlanta I used to frequent for beef ribs, the One Star Rib Ranch (used to be called the Lone Star Rib Ranch), owned and operated by a Texan, smokes them at 175° F for 12 to 13 hours, and they are *so* good, they just fall off the bone and melt in your mouth! One beef rib is a whole dinner! You could barely finish two of them, that's for sure. If you've got big eyes, they'll bring you three, and you'll sit there sucking on those ribs all night! I can taste them now. Atlanta has some good ribs, boy! And my favorite two places are little rib joints, not chains or restaurants. That's how it ought to be! But you can do this at home with proper meat, time, and preparation.

Owen Hart . . . King of the Ribbers!

Many years ago World Wrestling Federation offered our fans the opportunity to go on a cruise with the Superstars, and one of the Superstars on this trip was the late Owen Hart. As many will remember, Owen died on Sunday, May 23, 1999, in Kansas City during a Pay-Per-View event in Kemper Arena, after accidentally falling from the rafters attempting a spectacular ring entrance. Without a doubt this was the saddest day of my professional life, and it is a story I will tell in depth at another time. To this very day I have never watched a tape of that broadcast, but I will make myself watch it again before I attempt to capture my thoughts in words about the tragedy. However, my fondest memories were of the fun-loving, always smiling youngest of the twelve children of Stu and Helen Hart, Owen, who was the greatest ribber for my money in the history of wrestling.

It was the second day of the cruise and we were at sea, with many of us hanging around the pool and hopping in it to cool off every few minutes. My portly frame is certainly better suited for air-conditioning, and to say I was sweating Crisco that hot day would be an understatement, so I spent more time in the cool water than most. Several of the wrestlers' wives, including my own, were taking it easy in their deck chairs, enjoying the sun and watching their children, who were playing in the shallow end of the pool. Fans were also seated everywhere, enjoying their once-in-a-lifetime opportunity to mingle and get to know the Superstars in a most unique

Here, the late Owen Hart and I are broadcasting a WWE event in Sun City, South Africa. He's probably playing "ribs" in Heaven as we speak.

environment. Little did I know but Owen had entered the pool behind me. The "audience" saw him, but ol' J.R. did not. All of a sudden down came my swimsuit all the way to my ankles! I was damned near naked, as my ample-sized attire was now around my feet. I panicked! One foot came out of my suit! As *Seinfeld*'s George Costanza once bemoaned, there was *significant shrinkage!* Owen's audience was shocked, and so was I. It was no sight for the women and children to witness, but the damage had been done. I regrouped, so to speak, and finally pulled my trunks back to their proper place, but I had been had! The victim of an Owen Hart–orchestrated rib! Everyone laughed, but no one laughed louder than Owen. The rascal had got me and got me good. I still chuckle to this day thinking about that moment and wish Owen was still here to play another one of his ribs on me. I miss him very much, but he always brings a smile to my face when I think about him.

There is nothing in the outdoor cooking world that is **more tasty** *than properly prepared ribs*

TOP **TEN** FOODS THE TALENT LIKES TO SEE AT THE BUFFET TABLE AT **WWE** EVENTS*

10 Good pie **9** Fresh fruit **8** Salad **7** Rice

6 Pasta **5** Homemade or good bakery bread

4 Baked or grilled fish

3 Chicken (especially *grilled* chicken breasts, but not dry or not cooked too long)

2 Steak

1 Any good local dish

*Quantity is a big thing with these food-eating machines.

Let's start the day off right with some great breakfasts, as the opening matchup of foods of the day

THERE'S BELL

THE

SERVES 3 J.R.'S AWESOME SCRAMBLED EGGS (SEE WHAT EVERYONE IS TALKING ABOUT)

6 eggs

⅓ cup milk

1 tsp. dried chives

½ tsp. seasoned salt

1 tbsp. butter

salt and pepper to taste

1 In bowl *add* eggs, milk, chives, seasoned salt and beat until mixed well.

2 In a cast-iron skillet *melt* 1 tbsp. butter on medium heat.

3 *Scramble* eggs. Serve, add salt and pepper to taste.

WILD, WILD WESTERN

SERVES 1

3 tbsp. Monterey Jack cheese, cut into cubes or grated

1 tbsp. chives, dried or fresh

2 eggs

2 tbsp. milk

1 tbsp. butter

¼ cup chopped onion

¼ cup chopped green bell pepper

6 tbsp. diced cooked ham or Canadian bacon

salt and pepper, to taste

1 *Combine* in small bowl cheese and chives.

2 In another bowl combine eggs and milk. Lightly *beat*.

3 Melt butter in 10-inch nonstick skillet. Add onion, bell pepper, and ham. *Stir* over medium heat for about 2 minutes.

4 Raise the heat to medium high and add egg mixture. Cook until omelet bubbles around the edges, then stir, gathering the mixture to center of the pan. Cook until set, and then add cheese and chive mixture and salt and pepper. Cook until the filling is heated through, about half a minute or so. Slide the omelet halfway onto a plate, then *flip over* and serve immediately.

RISE-AND-SHINE GRANOLA

2 cups natural raisin and nut granola cereal

2 cups flavored or plain yogurt

sliced strawberries, peaches or blueberries

1 In a medium bowl, *top* the granola with yogurt.

2 *Divide* the cereal between two or three bowls and top with your choice of fruits.

C E R E A L

SERVES 2 TO 3

J.R.'S FAMOUS FRIED POTATOES

3 medium potatoes, washed, scrubbed, and diced

1 medium red onion or Vidalia, chopped

½ tsp. seasoned salt, or to taste

¼ tsp. salt

¼ tsp. pepper

1 tbsp. olive oil

Heinz ketchup (optional)

1 In large skillet, *heat* oil over medium-low heat. Add potatoes, onion, salts, and pepper. Stirring frequently, sauté until potatoes are soft and onion is translucent, about 10 minutes.

2 Cover and *cook* on low for 10 minutes.

3 Remove cover and cook until *browned* and crispy.

4 *Serve* with ketchup if desired.

SERVES 4

SERVES 6 RAISIN BREAD FRENCH TOAST—

4 eggs

¾ cup milk

½ tsp sugar

1 tsp cinnamon

pinch of nutmeg

8 slices of raisin bread

3 tbsp butter

Aunt Jemima Lite maple syrup

1 Combine eggs, milk, sugar, cinnamon, and nutmeg in a bowl and whisk to *blend*. Dip bread in egg mixture, covering both sides.

2 In nonstick skillet over medium heat, *melt* 1 tbsp. butter and cook bread 4 to 5 minutes on each side or until lightly browned. Repeat with other slices, adding remaining butter, as needed.

3 *Serve* with maple syrup.

TEXAS-SIZED

QUICK CINNAMON

ROLLS

3 tbsp. sugar

⅓ tsp. salt

2 tbsp. butter

¼ cup warm water

I egg, slightly beaten

I ¼-oz. pkg. dry yeast

2–2½ cups flour

½ cup butter or margarine

I tsp. cinnamon or Cinnabon cinnamon

⅓ cup dark brown sugar

½ cup raisins (optional)

1 In medium bowl *dissolve* sugar, salt, and 2 tbsp. butter in warm water. Add egg and yeast. Mix with flour.

2 *Roll* dough on a floured board to 8 inches by 8 inches to ¾ inch thick.

3 Melt ½ cup of butter and add cinnamon, brown sugar, and raisins. Mix well and *spread* on top of the dough. Roll up and cut ¾ inch thick. Put in a nonstick pan and let rise about 45 minutes to 1 hour. Bake at 350° F for 15–20 minutes in a greased pan or until browned.

MY PLANE RIDE WITH THE "MICK" . . . NOT FOLEY, MANTLE

It was 1987, and **Cowboy Bill Watts** sold the UWF (Universal Wrestling Federation) to Jim Crockett Promotions, and the headquarters of the merged companies was located in Dallas, Texas. My announce services were retained by the Crockett's and I moved from Bixby, Oklahoma, to Big D to start my new job. I had just bought a new Lincoln and packed my belongings in the car. They all fit nicely after my divorce, and I headed to Texas to start a new chapter in my life and career.

However, for the previous fifteen or so years I had officiated Oklahoma high school football with the same basic crew every Friday night in high schools all over the eastern part of the state, and prior to the sale we had finalized our schedule. I decided that since I had made the commitment to my crew to work the season's games that I would fly up to Oklahoma every Friday afternoon, rent a vehicle, and join my crew of **Dr. Dan Fuller, Ron Cox, and Charlie Wilson** for our last season together. My late father was big on keeping one's word. Commitment was a big thing around my house growing up. So even though I lost money every weekend—the pay for officiating was only about fifty to sixty dollars per game—I would purchase a plane ticket, rent a car, get a hotel room, and enjoy our final season together. Because I needed to travel cost efficiently and on a carrier I could depend on, I became a regular passenger on Southwest Airlines.

OU Sooners, Mickey Mantle and John Wayne adorn my office walls at WWE headquarters. A bottle of my BBQ Sauce would make this photo perfect.

One Friday, I am on my regular flight and have taken my seat in the first boarding group. There are no seat assignments on Southwest, and who comes and sits beside me but my boyhood hero, one of the greatest baseball players of all time and fellow Oklahoman, **Mickey Mantle!** I almost wet my pants! The Mick was sitting right next to good ol' J.R. I could not believe my eyes. And believe it or not, Mick knew who I was! He knew wrestler Wahoo McDaniel from their infamous golf games together and had watched my work occasionally on SuperStation TBS out of Atlanta. We had a great chat about each of us growing up in eastern Oklahoma, Mick in Commerce and me in Westville. The Mick had three beverages, all screwdrivers as I recall, on the forty-minute flight to Tulsa, where he was going to sign autographs at a baseball card show. When I told him what I was doing he said, "Do you make any money doing those games?"

"No, sir," was my answer. The Mick sat there a moment and gazed at the beautiful young blonde Southwest flight attendant in khaki shorts walking down the aisle and then a smile came over his face.

"Now I get it. You must have a girlfriend or two in good ol' Oklahoma which makes the trip worthwhile for you. I knew you were smarter than you looked!" And then he slapped me on the leg and laughed, saying, "A man after my own heart." Mickey must have signed two dozen autographs on the flight, but believe it or not, I never asked for one for myself, and to this day I can't tell you why. Since that time I have become an avid collector of Mickey Mantle memorabilia and am now the proud owner of a **1951 Bowman**

Mantle rookie baseball card in mint condition worth more money today than my daddy paid for the farm I grew up on. I also have dozens of Mantle-autographed baseballs, gloves, bats, caps, jerseys, and photos, including the covers, all autographed, of every *Sports Illustrated* on which Mick ever appeared. Though I have no autograph from our airplane flight together, I still have a memory that will last a lifetime.

a new chapter in

my life and career

Good groceries

are a necessity

for lunch!

SANDWICHES
AND BURGERS

WRESTLEMANIA BURGER!

1 ½ lb. ground sirloin or 80% lean ground chuck

1 tsp. garlic powder or salt

2 dashes Worcestershire sauce, or to taste

½ cup grated onion

sea salt and pepper to taste

4 Martin's potato hamburger buns

lite mayonnaise to taste

Heinz ketchup or Heinz hamburger relish to taste

4 slices red onion, or Vidalia

4 slices tomato

4 lettuce leaves

1 Combine ground sirloin, garlic powder, Worcestershire sauce, onion, sea salt and pepper and *mix* well.

2 *Form* into four equal patties.

3 Grill 5–10 minutes on *medium high* on each side until desired doneness and making sure it is not pink inside.

4 Spread mayonnaise, ketchup or relish, *top* with onion, tomato, and lettuce.

MAKES 4 BURGERS

J.R.'S TIP—*May top with J.R.'s BBQ Sauce. Can't find it in your store? Order from wwe.com. Click on Shopzone.*

TOP TEN BEST FOREIGN CITIES TO EAT IN

10 Bangalore, India (only kidding)

9 Berlin

8 Mexico City

7 Johannesburg, South Africa

6 Vancouver

5 London

4 Tokyo

3 Dublin

2 Toronto

1 Montreal

FLAME-GRILLED PORTABELLO MUSHROOM BURGER

4 whole portabello mushrooms (stems removed)

flavored oil such as oregano, basil, thyme, or rosemary

4 hamburger buns

salt and pepper

1 *Prepare* gas grill or charcoal grill to medium heat.

2 Place washed portabello caps on a dish and *brush* both sides with oil.

3 Grill the caps top side down 2–4 minutes. Gently turn and lower heat if necessary. *Grill* 1–2 minutes longer. Turn.

4 You may *toast* the hamburger buns during the last minutes of cooking, if desired.

5 *Season* with salt and pepper and serve.

MAKES 4 BURGERS

CHAR-GRILLED

1 16-oz. package Nathan's beef hot dogs (8 dogs)

Martin's potato hot dog buns

1 Place pierced hot dogs on medium-high heat and grill about 8 minutes total, or to your liking. *Grill* buns for 1 minute and choose from J.R.'s favorite toppings.

HOT DOG!

MAKES 8 DOGS

J.R.'S TIP—*If you want to get the best grilled hot dogs in the world, you need to go to Swanky Franks in Norwalk, Connecticut.*

TOP TEN THINGS THAT WOULD

10 I dislike corn on the cob, but I love corn bread.

9 The smell of Jack Daniel's bourbon makes me just a little bit queasy. (You can figure out why.)

8 I once used "Mr. L." cologne to attempt to eliminate beer breath at age fifteen. (It didn't work, by the way.)

7 My first vehicle was a '55 Chevy that I paid $300 for in 1967.

6 My second vehicle was a '57 Chevy that I paid $700 for in 1968 after the '55 Chevy fell apart.

5 I once went one-on-one in football with my dad in our living room at age sixteen, resulting in a chipped tooth and a cracked rib for yours truly. The old man came out unscathed.

4 My mom and dad never missed one of my football games, and to my dismay I never thanked them.

SURPRISE YOU ABOUT J.R.

3 I'm still angry at Bruce Dern for killing John Wayne In the movie *The Cowboys.*

2 I attended Major League Umpire School in 1976 and officiated high school and college football, basketball, and baseball for over fifteen years, including fourteen Oklahoma High School State Championship games.

1 I was state vice president of the Future Farmers of America in Oklahoma and the state FFA Speech Champion in 1968. I still have my blue and gold jacket, but it's a little tight.

JUST LIKE AT THE FAIR

MAKES 8 DOGS

CORN DOGS

¾ cup self-rising flour

¼ cup Quaker yellow cornmeal

2 tbsp. grated onion

1 tbsp. sugar

1 tsp. dry mustard

½ cup milk

1 egg beaten

1-lb. package Boar's Head hot dogs

vegetable oil

Popsicle sticks

1 *Heat* griddle.

2 Mix flour, cornmeal, onion, sugar, mustard, milk, and egg in a large bowl. Mix well. Pat dry hot dogs and push a Popsicle stick up into each hot dog, leaving 2 inches showing. *Dip* in batter mixture and add oil to fry pan or griddle. Heat oil to 350° F–375° F. Cook for 2–3 minutes or until well browned.

3 Remove, grabbing stick with tongs. *Drain* on paper towels and serve with favorite condiments.

J.R.'S TIP—*Always be careful when frying with grease, as it splatters. Keeping a bowl of cool water with ice in it to treat burns is a wise precaution.*

HEALTHY & TASTY

1 12-to-16-oz. package turkey bacon

½ small head lettuce

8 slices Martin's potato bread or white bread

4 ripe tomatoes

lite Miracle Whip or lite mayonnaise

In medium skillet on medium-low heat place turkey bacon strips and cook 5 minutes on each side. Place paper towels on plate. Remove strips from pan and drain on paper towel. *Slice* tomatoes and lettuce. Toast bread and make sandwiches with mayonnaise.

TURKEY BLTs

MAKES 4 SANDWICHES

SMOKEHOUSE TURKEY REUBEN SANDWICHES

½ **cup lite mayonnaise or lite salad dressing**

¼ **cup Heinz chili sauce**

1¼ **tbsp. Heinz sweet pickle relish**

8 **slices rye bread or seedless rye**

¼ **cup butter, softened**

½ **lb. lite Swiss cheese, grated**

½ **lb. smoked turkey, sliced**

1 **cup well-drained sauerkraut**

1   *Mix* mayonnaise, chili sauce, and relish in a small bowl. Set aside.

2   Take two slices of bread and lightly *butter* each on one side.

3   *Set* butter side down in a large nonstick frying pan or griddle.

4   Spread the bread with mayonnaise mix, then top with one-quarter of the cheese, *spreading* evenly with turkey and sauerkraut.

5   *Butter* two slices and place on top of sandwich butter side up.

6   Place over medium heat. *Press* gently on top of each sandwich with spatula until the underside is golden, approximately 4 minutes.

7   Carefully turn the sandwich over and repeat until the cheese has melted. *Flip* 2 more times to cook through, 1 or 2 minutes.

8   *Transfer* to individual plates. Repeat and cook 2 more sandwiches.

9   *Serve* immediately.

J.R.'S TIP—*If you'd like to reduce the fat, you may omit the cheese.*

MAKES 4 SANDWICHES

SOUTHWEST
SERVES 4 # CHICKEN

QUESADILLAS

1 10-oz. pkg. Perdue ready cooked chicken

½ cup onions, sliced

½ tsp. seasoned salt and pepper, to taste

4 10-inch flour tortillas

8 oz. lite Monterey Jack cheese, shredded

4 tbsp. Santa Fe Salsa (page 88)

chopped cilantro, to taste

low-fat sour cream

Pam nonstick spray

coarse ground pepper, to taste

1 Spray Pam in a medium pan over medium heat, and add chicken and onion until lightly sautéed or onions are translucent, adding seasoned salt and pepper. Set aside. *Spray* another nonstick pan with Pam, and place over medium-high heat. Place a tortilla in the pan and sprinkle with ¼ of the cheese and top with ¼ of the chicken mixture and 1 tbsp. of the salsa. Fold the tortilla in half and press with spatula. Cook for about 2 minutes, turn, and cook the second side about 1 minute. Repeat with remaining tortillas. Cut into triangles and serve hot. Garnish with cilantro and serve with extra salsa and sour cream.

I NEVER KNEW JOHN WAYNE, BUT I DID MEET DICK BUTKUS

My daddy loved **John Wayne** movies and watched every one he could when one would come on our small black-and-white television set in our four-room concrete block house in rural, eastern Oklahoma. The "Duke" represented America to my late father. The Duke was a man's man, and so was Daddy. My love today of John Wayne is a direct result of the memories I have of the late J.D. Ross, my father. I have collected John Wayne memorabilia for many years now, largely because of my wife, **Jan**, and proudly own one of the Duke's cigarette lighters, three pairs of his cuff links, one of which I wear every year at *WrestleMania,* one of his personally worn monogrammed shirts, and several autographed photos. I even bid for the Resistol hat he wore in his last movie, *The Shootist,* but got the limber tail when the bidding reached $31,000!

Unfortunately, I never got to meet John Wayne, but I did have the privilege of meeting and working with a man much like the Duke, former Chicago Bear and **NFL Hall of Famer Dick Butkus**. Dick fiercely competed on Sundays for the Monsters of the Midway in the Windy City and played middle linebacker, in my opinion, better than any man who ever lived. The Rock's pal, **linebacker Ray Lewis** of the Baltimore Ravens, is right up there today, but no one compares in my eyes to Number 51 of the Chicago Bears. Dick is a straight-shootin', tell-it-like-it-is, great American. His "old school" work ethic and passion for what he believes in was an inspiration for me during our season together broadcasting in the much maligned XFL football league. Let me tell you there are plenty of stories to tell of the XFL, but I will never forget being in the broadcast booth, preparing for our games, and sharing a cold beer with an American legend and great gridiron warrior. From where I sit, Dick Butkus is a viable part of the fabric of this country.

That's my story, and I'm sticking to it!

*Dick is a straight-shootin', tell-it-like-it-is, **great** American*

Condiments
and Sauces

*You can't have a great
meal without some sizzle!*

FIXIN'S

GRANDAD'S
MOONSHINE

MAKES 2½ CUPS

BBQ SAUCE

2 cups Heinz ketchup

½ cup light molasses

⅓ cup whiskey

2½ tbsp. Dijon mustard

1 tbsp. J.R.'s Hot Sauce

2 tbsp. Worcestershire sauce

2 tsp. paprika

1 tsp. garlic power

1 tsp. onion power

2 tsp. brown sugar (light or dark)

1 In a medium sauce pan, bring all ingredients to a *boil* over medium heat. Reduce heat to medium low and simmer approximately 15 minutes. Refrigerate.

J.R.'S TIP—*Keeps one week. You can get my hot sauce at wwe.com. Click on Shopzone.*

My great-grandpa Ross, a giant of a man at six foot seven and two-ninety, was a famous moonshiner in Adair County in the thirties.

POWERSLAM PICANTE SAUCE

9 medium tomatoes, peeled and diced

1½ cups onions, diced

1 12-oz. can tomato sauce

1 garlic clove, chopped

1½ cups green bell pepper, diced

½ cup vinegar

1½ tbsp. sugar

½ tbsp. black pepper

salt to taste

J.R.'s Hot Sauce to taste

1 small jalapeño pepper, seeded and diced

1 *Place* tomatoes, onions, jalapeño, and green peppers in large pot.

2 Add rest of ingredients and *adjust* seasonings to taste.

3 *Simmer* on low for 2 hours.

4 Place in ball jars and *seal*.

J.R.'S TIP—*When handling hot peppers, use rubber or plastic gloves (you can buy disposable latex gloves in any drugstore) to protect your hands, and avoid touching your face.*

J.R. AND JAN'S MACARONI AND CHEESE

SERVES 8

1 lb. small shaped pasta, like elbows or penne

4 cups milk

4 tbsp. butter

6 tbsp. flour

1 tsp. paprika

pinch of salt

pepper to taste

4 cups grated Gruyère cheese

3 tbsp. grated low-fat or regular cheddar cheese

1 *Preheat* oven to 350° F.

2 In a large pot, cook pasta following package directions. *Drain* and place in a large bowl.

3 Bring milk to a boil in another pan, set aside. Melt butter in another pan. Add flour slowly to butter, whisking over a low heat for 5 minutes. Avoid browning. Remove from heat. Add milk to butter-flour mixture and blend well. Add ½ tsp. paprika, and salt and pepper, to taste. Return pan to heat. *Cook* over a medium heat, stirring constantly, about 5 minutes, until thickened. Pour over pasta and mix thoroughly.

4 Butter a 13-x-9-x-2 baking dish and fill with prepared pasta. Sprinkle grated Gruyère cheese, remaining paprika, and pepper over top. Place dish on a foil-covered baking sheet. Bake for 20–25 minutes. Remove from oven and turn the oven up to broil. *Sprinkle* cheddar cheese evenly over the top and place under broiler, with the rack on the lowest setting, for 3–4 minutes, or until slightly golden. Serve hot.

SOUTHERN-STYLE SMOKED BRISKET

MAKES 2½ CUPS

SAUCE

3 tbsp. vegetable oil

1 onion, chopped

1 stalk celery chopped

2 cloves garlic, minced

1½ tbsp. chili powder

1½ tbsp. brown sugar

1 tbsp. dried oregano

1½ tsp. paprika

1 bay leaf

¾ cup low-sodium beef broth

½ cup Heinz chili sauce

½ cup Heinz ketchup

¼ cup Heinz apple cider vinegar

2 tbsp. Worcestershire sauce

¾ tsp. J.R.'s Hot Sauce

1 In medium saucepan *heat* oil and sauté onion, celery, and garlic over medium heat for about 5 minutes until soft, stirring constantly.

2 Add chili powder, brown sugar, oregano, and paprika and cook 1 minute. *Add* bay leaf, beef broth, chili sauce, apple cider vinegar, Worcestershire sauce, and Hot Sauce. Bring to a boil, then reduce heat to low. Simmer for 20 minutes until thickened.

OKLAHOMA RANCH DRESSING

1 cup buttermilk

1⅓ cup lite mayonnaise

¼ cup lite sour cream

1 tbsp. parsley flakes

1 tsp. salt

⅛ tsp. white pepper

1 small clove garlic, minced

1 tsp. finely grated onion

1 *Mix* all ingredients well and store, for up to 3 days, covered in the refrigerator.

MAKES 2½ CUPS

AUNT JANE'S POTATO SALAD

6 medium potatoes

1½ tsp. salt

¾ cup celery, sliced

½ cup red onion, chopped fine

⅓ cup sweet pickles, coarsely chopped

1 cup low-fat mayonnaise or salad dressing

2 tsp. sugar

2 tsp. celery seed

1 tsp. pimento, chopped

1 tsp. yellow (hot dog) mustard

1½ tsp. salt

3 hard-boiled eggs, chopped

Fill a medium saucepan three-quarters of the way with water and cover. Bring water to a boil. Add potatoes and ½ tsp. salt. Boil for 30 minutes. Drain well, and let cool. *Peel* and cube the potatoes. Place potatoes in large bowl. Add celery, onion, and sweet pickles, toss. In a small bowl combine mayonnaise, sugar, celery seed, pimento, mustard, and salt. Add to potato mixture. Gently fold in eggs. Cover and refrigerate.

"THE BEST EVER MADE"

SERVES 6-8

TOP TEN UNUSUAL THINGS J.R. HAS SEEN AT RINGSIDE

10 NFL stars totally suspending their disbelief and having fun like regular folks.

9 Siegfried and Roy look-alikes. (It either must have been around Halloween or Las Vegas.)

8 Some of Hollywood's biggest stars, like Dennis Hopper, Nick Cage, Dennis Miller, Rob Reiner, Andy Richter, Susan Sarandon, and Michael Clarke Duncan having a great time with other WWE fans.

7 HLA.

6 Small children dressed as wrestlers, including the obligatory tattoos. There's nothing like seeing a three-year-old flipping the bad guy "the bird" à la Stone Cold!

5 A Seeing Eye dog eating popcorn and drinking beer with his owner.

4 Large women fighting. (There's nothing like seeing two 300-pounders go at it in Wisconsin. Ah . . . cheese!)

3 MANY topless women (King's favorite).

2 A mom breast-feeding her child at ringside. (This did not make air, and I laid off milk for at least a week.)

1 A man proposing to his lady and inviting J.R. to the wedding. (I couldn't make it, but I would have sent a gift!)

TRUE GRITS ...

6 cups water

1½ cups quick grits

1½ sticks butter

1 lb. grated low-fat or regular cheddar cheese

2 tbsp. salt

3 eggs beaten

1 Preheat oven to 350° F.

2 In large saucepan, bring the water to a boil.

3 Add grits and cook uncovered for 10 minutes.

4 Remove from heat and add cheese, salt, and eggs.

5 Place in an 8-by-10 baking dish and bake at 350° F for 1½ hours.

6 Serve immediately.

PILGRAM

SERVES 6

MAKES ABOUT 5 CUPS

MAMA'S CHOW CHOW

1 lb. green tomatoes

¾ lb. red tomatoes

½ green pepper

½ red pepper

1 medium onion

1 jalapeño pepper seeded

1 tbsp. salt

2 cups Heinz apple cider vinegar

1¼ cups sugar

1 Finely *chop* tomatoes and onion. Seed and finely chop bell peppers and jalapeño.

2 Place chopped vegetables, salt, vinegar and sugar in pot and bring to a *boil* stirring occasionally.

3 *Cook* for 30–40 minutes over medium high heat until thickened.

4 Allow to *cool* before serving.

5 *Store* in the refrigerator.

J.R.'S TIP—*Try it on everything—be creative!*
Can store up to 2 weeks.

PURPLE ONION

MARINADE

2 tbsp. lemon juice

¼ cup vegetable oil

½ tsp. sea salt

⅛ tsp. coarse ground black pepper

1 small purple onion chopped

1 *Combine* all ingredients in a mixing bowl and let stand for 30 minutes.

2 Serve over *tossed* salad or mesclun salad.

MAKES ABOUT ¾ CUP

GRILLED RED ONIONS

4 small purple onions

I tbsp. olive oil

Lawry's season salt to taste

salt and pepper, to taste

1 *Heat* grill to medium.

2 Peel onions. Cut aluminum foil into 8-x-8-inch squares. Coat each onion with oil and season with season salt, salt, and pepper. Place onion in center of the square and seal. *Cook* over medium heat until desired doneness.

3 Let cool, then make an X in center and *fill* with your favorite tuna, chicken, or shrimp salad.

SERVES 4

DANDY HERB-BUTTERMILK

MARINADE

1 cup buttermilk

¾ tbsp. Dijon mustard

1 tbsp. honey

½ tbsp. fresh rosemary, minced or dried

½ tsp. dried thyme

½ tsp. dried sage

½ tsp. dried majoram

1 tsp. sea salt

½ tsp. coarse ground pepper

1 In a medium bowl, *blend* together all ingredients. Refrigerate.

MAKES 1 CUP

J.R.'S TIP—*Keeps one week. Great on chicken and pork.*

SOUTHWESTERN-STYLE BBQ RUB

MAKES ABOUT ¼ CUP, ENOUGH FOR 2½-3 LBS. OF STEAK

2 tsp. coarse ground pepper

1 tbsp. paprika

1 tsp. light brown sugar

1½ tsp. garlic powder

1 tsp. sea salt

¼ tsp. cayenne

2 tsp. mustard seeds, crushed

Pam olive oil

1 In a medium bowl *stir* together all ingredients.

2 *Rub* onto steaks and spray with Pam and let stand at room temperature for 30 minutes, or refrigerate for 3–4 hours before grilling.

J.R.'S TIP—*Try this on ribeye, strip steaks, t-bone, or porterhouse.*

SWEET-AND-SPICY CHILI

MAKES ABOUT ¾ CUP

KETCHUP

- ½ cup Heinz ketchup
- 1 tbsp. Worcestershire sauce
- 1 tbsp. red wine vinegar
- 1 tbsp. brown sugar
- 1 tsp. chili powder
- 1 tsp. minced onion
- ½ tsp. coarse ground pepper
- ¼ cup water

1 In a small saucepan, *whisk* together all ingredients.

2 *Simmer* over low heat approximately 10 minutes.

3 Allow to cool, then *transfer* to a bowl for storage. Refrigerate. Keeps two weeks.

J.R.'S TIP—*Recipe may be doubled.*
Great as a dipping sauce for steaks, eggs, or meat loaf.

SERVES 8–10

SANTA FE SALSA

4 medium ripe tomatoes, diced

½ cup celery, chopped

½ cup red onion, chopped

½ cup canned green chiles, drained

⅛ tsp. garlic salt

2 drops Worcestershire sauce

1 tsp. white vinegar

⅛ tsp. oregano, dried

3 drops J.R.'s Hot Sauce

3 tbsp. cilantro

I *Mix* all ingredients in a medium bowl and refrigerate for 1½ hours. Serve with your favorite tortilla chips.

UNCLE MITCH'S

COLESLAW

1 medium head green cabbage

¾ cup low-fat mayonnaise or Miracle Whip

½ cup milk

sugar, to taste

½ tsp. salt

pinch of pepper

1 carrot peeled and grated

1 small onion grated

1 Cut and finely shred cabbage. In large bowl mix mayonnaise, milk, sugar, salt, and pepper, blend well. Then add cabbage, carrots, and onions. *Toss* to coat with dressing. Cover and store in refrigerator for 3 hours.

SERVES 6

"This was the first-prize winner at the Adair County Fair. That's another one of my stories, and I'm sticking to it!"

OLD-FASHIONED TURKEY GRAVY

¼ cup drippings from roasted turkey pan

6 tbsp. flour

4 cups chicken broth or milk

salt and pepper

Place drippings in medium saucepan over medium heat, and gradually add 6 tbsp. flour, *whisking* until it forms a smooth paste. Slowly add 4 cups of broth or milk, whisking constantly, then reduce heat to low and simmer for about 20 minutes. The gravy will thicken. Stir often. As gravy simmers, season with salt and pepper to taste. Serve warm.

MAKES 4 CUPS

COUNTRY WHITE GRAVY

3 tbsp. poultry drippings (may use bacon or sausage also)

¾ cup milk

3 tbsp. flour

1 tsp. salt

dash pepper

¾–1 cup milk

1 Place drippings in medium skillet. In a jar with a tight-fitting lid, or a small bowl, combine ¾ cup milk, flour, salt, and pepper. Shake until well combined in jar or mix thoroughly in bowl. On medium heat, stir into drippings. *Cook*, stirring constantly until desired consistency. It should be thick and bubbly. Add additional milk if necessary.

MAKES 1½ CUPS

J.R.'S TIP—*Great over hot homemade biscuits!*

HOMEMADE APPLE BUTTER

1½ lbs. McIntosh apples, peeled and cored

1½ cups apple cider

⅛ cup honey

¼ cup light brown sugar

½ tsp. ground cinnamon

⅛ tsp. allspice

pinch of cloves

5 red hots

1 Place apples and cider in a medium saucepan and bring to a boil. Reduce heat and simmer for about 10–15 minutes. *Stir* in remaining ingredients and cook for 20–40 minutes or until sauce becomes thick. Cool, then place into a food processor and process until smooth.

"Makes the world champ of pb&j's!"

MAKES ABOUT 2 CUPS

AUNT DEE'S THREE-DAY

CARROTS

2 lbs. carrots, peeled and cut into 3-inch strips

1 10-oz. can Campbell's tomato soup

⅓ cup vegetable oil

¾ cup white vinegar

1 cup sugar

1 tsp. salt

2 medium onions, sliced

1 medium green pepper, seeded and sliced into
   strips or rings

1 In a large pot place carrots and add just enough water to cover. Cook carrots over a medium heat for 10–12 minutes until tender. Drain and cool. In a large glass bowl **combine** carrots with remaining ingredients and stir. Cover and store in a cool dry place for 3 days. Serve.

MAKES 6-8 SERVINGS

J.R.'S TIP—*Can keep up to two weeks.*

CHARLES BARKLEY
SHOULD, AT THE VERY LEAST, BE GOVERNOR OF
ALABAMA!

I consider former NBA great, and current broadcaster, **Charles Barkley** to be a friend of mine *and* one of the smartest men I know. Charles is known as one of the most outspoken people on television with his oftentimes outrageous remarks during NBA telecasts. I personally know Charles to be one of the most generous, bighearted individuals I have ever met. He is also a fan of WWE, and he enjoys J.R. and the King's commentary on *Raw,* which he has said many times makes him laugh out loud.

A few years ago after a live *Raw* in Phoenix, the King and his then-fiancée, **Stacy "the Kat" Carter**, along with my wife, Jan, and I hooked up with Sir Charles and went to dinner at one of his favorite spots in town. We talked about his family, him growing up in Alabama, which for a black man has never been a layup, no pun intended, his NBA days, his friendship with Michael Jordan and Tiger

Woods, his love of golf, gambling, women, and what his family has meant to him in his oftentimes controversial life.

Charles also loved to hear the stories from the King and me about our careers in our wacky profession. Just as he did for those in his life, he genuinely cared about ours. He may beat me up for saying this, but **Charles Barkley** is a sensitive, caring man who loves doing things for people. Charles actually paid for the King and Stacy's Las Vegas wedding, even though he was unable to attend because of a previous commitment. All who attended got the royal treatment, thanks to Sir Charles. In my view, he has become the best basketball commentator in the business because he is honest, and he genuinely cares about the game of basketball. I think I can relate to that philosophy. I can also say I think I have learned more about race issues because of Charles's insight, wisdom, and life experiences than anyone I have ever known, with the possible exception of **Ernie "The Big Cat" Ladd**. The great state of Alabama could do one helluva lot worse than having my friend Charles Barkley for governor, even though he would have to take a huge cut in pay!

SAUTÉED CINNAMON APPLES

1 28-oz. jar or 1 10-oz. can fried apples or

3 fresh apples, cored and sliced

1 tsp. cinnamon

1 tbsp. sugar

1 tbsp. butter (if using fresh apples)

1 Place apples in medium skillet on medium-low heat. Add sugar and cinnamon. If using fresh apples, melt butter in pan and then add apples, cinnamon, and sugar. Heat until apples are soft.

SERVES 3 – 4

HERE ARE SOME OF J.R.'S FAVORITE TOPPINGS

J.R.'s BBQ Sauce*

Chili with beans (or without)

Grilled onions

Cilantro

Coleslaw

Chopped garlic

Chopped green onions

J.R.'s Hot Sauce*

Jalapeños

Chopped Vidalia onion

Chow-Chow

Heinz ketchup

Mushrooms

Heinz mustard

Onion rings

Red onion slices

Pizza sauce

Bush's country pork & beans

Ranch dressing

Refried beans

Picante sauce

Heinz hamburger relish

Olives, green or black

Salsa

Sauerkraut (cold or hot)

Heinz sweet pickle relish

Tomatoes, or cherry tomatoes

Cheese dip

Green peppers

Lite sour cream

* Can't find them in your store? Order them from wwe.com. Click on Shopzone.

TOP **TEN** ARENAS
FOR BEST CATERING

10 Hartford, CT—fresh cooked pasta where the aroma of garlic fills the arena!

9 Baltimore, MD—best crab balls in the country!

8 Greensboro, NC—lots of homemade country cooking and "sweet" tea!

7 Austin, TX—where they serve up **BBQ** from Rudy's. Wrestlers love to "compete" after eating the baked beans, à la *Blazing Saddles*.

6 New York City's Madison Square Garden—great meat loaf, believe it or not!

5 Pittsburgh's Mellon Arena—juicy roast beef and great Italian food.

4 San Antonio, TX—Mexican food *and* BBQ! How do you beat that?

3 Knoxville, TN—turkey and dressing! Just like Granny used to make.

2 Lafayette, LA (Cajun Dome)— Cajun cookin' that would make the late Justin Wilson proud, including bread pudding.

1 Milwaukee (Bradley Center)—*Wow!* From homemade pasta to a huge selection of fresh salads, desserts to die for, all served with a smile.

TOP TEN CITIES FOR BEST CROWD RESPONSE*

10 Detroit, MI

9 Minneapolis, MN

8 London, England

7 Tokyo, Japan

6 Boston, MA

5 Oklahoma City

4 Toronto, Canada

3 Seattle, WA

2 New York (Madison Square Garden)

1 Chicago, IL

* Crowd response is strictly dependent on how good a product we provide our audience.

A NIGHT WHEN HOLLYWOOD'S "A" LIST ATTENDED *RAW*

The **Arrowhead Pond** in Anaheim, California, has always been a great spot for *WWE Raw* and is one of my personal favorites for the live, flagship broadcast of the company to emanate from. The Southern California fans usually provide a great deal of emotion to our broadcasts, and if we do our job of providing them a good product to experience *live,* they always let the world watching at home on TV know that they are having a great time. The early start, 6 P.M. Pacific time, is great for the talent and crew, as a rule, because we start the show with everyone fresher, and we finish earlier, which is a nice change. I have actually been able to get back to my hotel room in time to watch the West Coast feed of *Raw,* which is always interesting, especially if we have had a good night. Certainly another reason I enjoy doing *Raw* live from Anaheim, or L.A.'s Staples Arena for that matter, is you just never know what Hollywood-type celebrities will drop by to enjoy the show.

When we are in Southern California for *Raw,* I always ask one of our marketing reps who is coming from the world of movies, television, and sports. On one particular night, Paul Heyman and I had taken our places at ringside. (We are not positioned there any longer, by the way, but that's a story for another time.) About five minutes before we were to go live we glanced around the Pond, and it looked like a big Hollywood gathering of "A" list celebrities. You know the kind of get-together I'm referring to, a "my people will call your people"–type and we will tell each other how great we both are. Kind of like a reunion of former wrestling champions might be.

Anyway, we look around and there is Dennis Hopper, whose life would have made the late Brian Pillman's look like a walk on the beach. I think we suspended the great actor/director's disbelief that night, by the look I observed on his face—or maybe he had attended a preparty before the opening bell. Who knows? There was the multitalented Dennis Miller, who looked embarrassed when our cameras showed him there, even though he sure as hell seemed to be having a great time. I can relate a little to Miller, as he is a native of Pittsburgh, and so is my wife, and he got his Spauldings busted for his work on *Monday Night Football* much as I did for broadcasting *XFL Football.* At least Dennis got two seasons' worth of pay out of it. Nick Cage and his son were at ringside too and were loving every minute of *Raw* that night. They even came backstage and were very cordial and respectful of our business and our fans.

Most celebrities who attend our events are really regular folks, or at least they have come off that way to me. Probably the most regular (this sounds like a laxative ad) is our pal and Oscar winner for *The Green Mile,* Michael Clarke Duncan, who starred with The Rock in

The Scorpion King and absolutely loves WWE! We came very close, as a matter of fact, to having **The Rock** and Michael team for a WWE PPV in September of 2002, but their respective movie schedules posed scheduling problems. I have seen Michael so animated at our events that he even had to be restrained once from coming over the rail when The Rock was getting the boots put to him by an adversary.

We have always claimed that WWE is about entertaining our audiences, no different from what the aforementioned stars do for their audiences. The various Hollywood celebs who attend our events seem to appreciate and respect what the **WWE Superstars** do night in and night out, in a succession of one-night stands around the world. Each and every one of them know that performing before an audience on *live* television is the ultimate challenge.

performing before an
audience on live television
is the **ultimate** challenge

So Good They'll Make You Cry Like Your Best Hunting Dog Just Died

BREADS

FANTASTIC FRY BREAD

3 cups flour

I tbsp. baking powder

I tsp. salt

I tbsp. sugar

I cup water

vegetable oil

1 Mix dry ingredients in a large bowl. Add water. *Turn out* and knead lightly on floured surface. Roll into ½-inch-thick piece, then cut into 12 squares. Cut 2 slits in each square.

2 In a large pan, or cast-iron skillet, *fry* in vegetable oil on medium-high heat until browned.

3 *Drain* on paper towels.

SERVES 6

J.R.'S TIP—*Great served with pinto beans and/or honey.*

CAST-IRON COUNTRY

SERVES 6

CORN BREAD

2 cups Quaker yellow cornmeal

2 cups flour

1 cup sugar

2 tbsp. baking powder

1½ tsp. sea salt

2½ cups whole or 2% milk

1 cup vegetable oil

5 eggs

5 tbsp. butter

1 tbsp. honey

1 *Preheat* oven to 350° F. Grease a 13-x-9-x-2-inch pan.

2 In large bowl, stir cornmeal, flour, sugar, baking powder, and sea salt. Set aside. In another large bowl, beat together milk, oil, and eggs until blended well. Add the cornmeal/flour mixture and stir until just combined. Pour into **cast-iron skillet** or a prepared pan and bake for 40 minutes at 350° F. Cool and cut into 12 squares. Mix together butter and honey. Serve with corn bread.

J.R.'S TIP—*Great with pinto beans!*

HOT JALAPEÑO CORN BREAD

2 8½-oz. packages corn bread muffin mix

¾ cup onion, chopped fine

2 cups shredded lite cheddar cheese

1 14-oz. can cream-style corn, undrained

1½ cups lite sour cream

4 eggs, beaten

1 4-oz. can green chiles, drained and chopped

⅓ cup vegetable oil

jalapeño pepper, seeded and minced, to taste, or canned

1 Preheat oven to 350° F. *Grease* 13-x-9-x-2-inch baking dish.

2 In large bowl, combine corn bread mix and onion. Then add the remaining ingredients and combine. *Pour* into prepared dish and bake at 350° F for 40–50 minutes or until golden.

J.R.'S TIP—*When handling hot peppers, wear rubber or plastic gloves to protect hands, and avoid touching your face.*

SERVES 12-16

MAMA'S BISCUITS

3 cups self-rising flour

3 tbsp. Domino's extra fine sugar

¾ cup white shortening

1 cup milk

honey (optional)

1 Preheat oven to 400° F. *Lightly grease* a baking sheet. In a large bowl combine 2½ cups of the flour and sugar. Using a pastry cutter, cut shortening into flour mix until crumbly. Stir in milk a little at a time until the flour is moistened. Work the dough into a ball. Using the remaining flour to flour surface, turn out dough, knead dough. Cut 2-inch circles, using a biscuit cutter or a large glass. Place onto the baking sheet. Bake for 15 minutes until golden brown. Remove to wire rack to cool. Serve with honey.

MAKES 15

GRANNY'S HUCKLEBERRY BREAD

1 egg

1 stick (8 tbsp.) butter, at room temp.

1 cup sugar

2 cups self-rising flour

1 cup milk

1 tsp. vanilla

2 cups huckleberries or blueberries

Heat oven to 350° F. Stir egg, butter, and sugar together in medium bowl. Add 1 cup flour, milk and vanilla. *Sprinkle* remaining flour over berries to prevent them from sinking during baking in batter. Add floured berries to mixture. Put in 8-inch loaf pan and bake about 40 minutes until golden.

MAKES 1 LOAF

TEXAS GARLIC

TOAST

1 loaf of French or Italian bread

3–5 tbsp. butter, softened to room temperature

1 tsp. garlic powder

½ tsp. paprika

1 *Heat* grill to low.

2 Cut the loaf into 1-inch diagonal slices cutting to, but not through, the bottom of the crust. In a small bowl *combine* the butter, garlic powder, and paprika until well blended. Spread the butter mixture between every other slice of bread. Wrap loosely in heavy-duty foil. Place on edge of grill. Grill over low coals about 10 minutes or until heated through, turning frequently.

MAKES 6 SERVINGS

BOOMER BANANA

MAKES 1 LOAF

2 cups flour

1 tsp. baking soda

1 tsp. salt

¾ cup butter

2 eggs

1 tsp. vanilla

1½ cup sugar

1½ cup mashed banana

½ cup buttermilk

½ cup nuts, preferably walnuts, chopped (optional)

1 Heat oven to 350° F. In medium bowl, stir together flour, soda, and salt. *Cream* butter, eggs, and vanilla. Add sugar, bananas, and buttermilk. Mix well, then fold in nuts.

2 Pour into 8–9-inch greased loaf pan. *Bake* for 1 hour at 350° F.

MAMA'S STRAWBERRY

1½ cups flour

I cup sugar

2 tsp. cinnamon

½ tsp. baking soda

½ tsp. salt

¾ cup vegetable oil

2 eggs, beaten

I 10-oz. box frozen strawberries, thawed, drained,
   and chopped

¾ cup chopped pecans

1 Preheat oven to 350° F. *Grease* and flour 8–9-inch loaf pan.

2 In a large bowl, combine flour, sugar, cinnamon, soda, salt. Add oil
   and eggs and *mix* well. Add strawberries, pecans. Bake at 350° F for
   1½ hours.

MY MAIN EVENT WITH BELL'S PALSY

That's me thanking our fans for their support. They stood behind me through two bouts of Bell's palsy.

The first time that a lot of WWE fans heard about the affliction called Bell's palsy was when they heard that "good ol' J.R." had it. What is it? How did he get it?

Without getting too technical, Bell's palsy is a condition that causes the facial muscles to weaken, droop, or become paralyzed. Not a lot is known about the causes or cures. It can be brought on by stress or trauma and is not permanent, so the experts say. It is named for **Sir Charles Bell**, a Scottish surgeon who two hundred years ago studied the effects of this condition on the facial muscles. Experts say that about 1 out of every 5,000 people over the course of their life-time, and 40,000 Americans every year, are affected by this illness.

The symptoms come up on you very quickly. Most people either wake up to find they have Bell's palsy, like I did, or have symp-toms such as a dry eye or tingling around their lips that progress to a full case of Bell's palsy that same day. It is not contagious, and people with Bell's palsy can return to work and resume normal activity as soon as they feel up to it. That doesn't include people who talk on television for a living.

Experts say that approximately 50 percent of Bell's palsy patients will have essentially complete recoveries in a short time. Another 35 percent will have good recoveries in less than a year. I've had mine for more years than I like to think about now. Bell's palsy is best described as an event-based trauma to the cervical nerve that is either physical or stress related. They still don't know for sure, and the possibility of recurrence is as high as 10 to 20 percent. Unfortunately I was in that small percentage too, as I got it twice. Here's my story about how Bell's palsy kicked me in the face and put me on the sidelines.

It was Super Bowl Sunday and the Dallas Cowboys were playing the Buffalo Bills in Atlanta in the familiar confines of the **Georgia Dome.** Jan and I were living in Wilton, Connecticut, and it was as cold as an ex-mother-in-law's hug. Yes, even colder than the other side of the pillow. But what did I expect? It was Connecticut, and it was winter. I had been on the job for about nine months after moving up from Atlanta where I had been working for Ted Turner's WCW, broadcasting Atlanta Falcon football games and doing a radio talk show on WSB-AM in Atlanta.

So far, I had not really fit in too well. After all, I was the former lead-announcer from the enemy camp in Atlanta. I was from the south with a southern drawl, and this was a northeastern-based company.

Oh well, no hill for a stepper, as they say down south, and things were beginning to smooth out for me over time. The hardworking folks at the TV studio lead by Executive Producer **Kevin Dunn** (who never, by the way, get the credit they deserve for the successes the company has experienced), were beginning to accept me. They saw me as being a hardworking guy who loved the business, was never late for work, and would do whatever they wanted to the very best of my ability. Things looked like they were improving for me. No, I was not the lead announcer anymore. Vince was. No, I was not the backup or number two announcer. Gorilla Monsoon was. I had to be content to stand on the sidelines, wearing a cap and holding a clipboard and always ready to play if called upon. Like **John Fogerty** once sang, "Put me in, Coach, I'm ready to play!" Even being the "third team" announcer was better than attempting to exist in the old WCW. That was a nightmare, with all the political backbiting, the overt insecurities of WCW management, a lack of leadership from Ted's lackeys, and an overall lack of commitment from the top Turner brass for 'rasslin, as Ted used to call it. Ted loved his 'rasslin, but his white-collar, blue-blazer, red-power-tie-wearing soldiers were embarrassed to be associated with the product, even though it delivered some of the station's best TV ratings year after year. More on the Turner experience at another time, but let me tell you there are plenty of stories to tell on that front, including rampant illegal drug use, adultery, out-of-control egos, and overall gross mismanagement of the product and Ted's money. Ah, the memories . . . but back to my first battle with Bell's palsy.

Super Bowl Sunday had arrived, the Cowboys versus the Bills, and Jan was working as a flight attendant, or "airline goddess" if you will, for U.S. "Scare," as we used to call it. I was all set to watch the big game alone. She should be home about halftime if all went well.

I woke up that morning, ready to make my regular run to get a Sunday paper or two, grab something to eat, and get back for the world's longest pregame show, which obviously only a football fanatic could endure. When I got out of bed I felt strange (no jokes, please), like my face was asleep. I also had one helluva headache, migraine level. My hearing out of my left ear was amplified tremendously. I went to the bathroom and looked in the mirror and was more shocked than usual at what I saw! The entire left side of my face was hanging. I could not shut my left eye, nor would it blink. I thought I had had a stroke in my sleep. I was scared as hell. I was not sure what to do. I got in my car and drove to one of those 24-hour minor emergency clinics, which can be an adventure in itself, let me tell you. I got in to see a doctor of Middle-Eastern descent who diagnosed me as having "a cold in my face." What??!! Or maybe Lyme disease as the result of a tick bite. He said I would be okay in a day or two and not to worry. He said don't worry about the overwhelming headaches, the ultra-sensitive hearing issue, the fact that I could not close my left eye, or that it would not blink. Don't worry about the fact that my tongue was numb and that I couldn't taste anything and that I was a television announcer by trade and that all these issues could put me out of business. He said I'd be okay in a day or two.

I might as well have gone to a veterinarian (and maybe should have)! Jan got home and looks at me in shock as I tell her my story of the 24-hour medical clinic. I try to relax and watch the big game, but the noise was killing me, and my head never hurt so bad in my life, and let me tell you I have had some dandy hangovers in my day. The next day we went to a neurologist in Greenwich, who diagnosed that I had the most severe case of Bell's palsy that he had seen in years. No reason can accurately be given as to why people get it. It could be viral or it could be stress-induced. No one knows for sure, and there is no absolute cure. I would start physical therapy, which included acupuncture (I used David Letterman's acupuncturist in Connecticut, if anyone cares), electrical stimulation and massage to attempt to get the nerves to come back alive so I could blink, smile, chew, taste, hear normally, stop drooling like a baby . . . you get the picture.

About two weeks later, it was early February and snowing like crazy. It was a Friday and the phone rang. The head of human resources was a woman named Lisa Wolf. She called me and said that she and Vince wanted to see me in Vince's office that afternoon, but she wouldn't say why. So I shower, shave, the usual, and tried to make myself somewhat presentable in spite of my physical appearance and made the ten- to fifteen-mile drive to the office, which because of the snowstorm would take me about an hour. The long ride certainly gave me the opportunity to think about what this meeting could be for. Maybe they wanted to offer me words of encouragement and try to lift my spirits, as by now I had been unable to perform my duties for about two weeks. There were plenty of places to park in the usually crowded parking lot because the weather was so bad and most of the employees had gone home early. I parked my car and hopped on the elevator. I was so self-conscious about my looks that I truly did not want anyone to see me if at all possible, and I headed directly to the fourth floor and the boss's office. He and a raven-haired, rather large lady were waiting for me, and I was brought right in. The meeting lasted about five minutes.

"I have decided to go in another direction and you are not in my plans" was what I heard from the most powerful man in the history of our business.

That was it. I brought up that my contract had another three months left to go on it, which seemed to cause a distressed look on the HR lady's face. It was agreed that the company would honor my final three months and pay me for the ninety or so days. Wolf wanted to know if I wanted to go to her office and talk about the situation or if I wanted them to set up counseling for me. Counseling for what? For getting fired two weeks after suffering my first bout of Bell's palsy? Did she think I needed "couch time" to discuss my occupational loss with some total stranger? To talk about my dream job coming to an end? What I needed was to know why I was gone. I also needed the respect of the "godfather" of our business, and I apparently had neither.

On the way home and another hour's drive in the snow, I called my beloved little wife and told her the news. She was damn sure stronger than me. We had only been married four months and now our life was changing big-time and there was nothing either of us could do about it. She assured me that everything would be just fine, that we would get back on our feet and we would do it together. God, I am so lucky to be married to this tough, little Italian from Pittsburgh! In a span of less than one year, I had been dumped on in Atlanta by WCW, gotten married, obtained my dream job working with

**Many of my friends say I "overachieved"
when Jan and I got married. They were right.**

the most significant figure in the history of our industry, debuting at the event, *WrestleMania IX,* contracted a debilitating illness, gotten fired from my dream job without really knowing why, and was preparing to move back to Atlanta to try to put things back together. Whew! I refused to leave the business and I refused to stop wondering why I got fired at the worst possible time and in the worst circumstances I could personally imagine. I wanted back in the game that was a major part of my life. I will never forget these experiences, nor would I change any of them.

Over the years, Vince and I have often spoken about those challenging times and what happened. If you were to ask him today, he would tell you he made a mistake in how this matter was handled. He eventually saw how badly I wanted to work in his family's company and how dedicated I was and am to the business we both passionately love. The timing of my departure was not good, but it did not kill me. It did not break my spirit or lessen my love for the wrestling business. I fought back through the Bell's palsy and I got my job back.

Vince McMahon and yours truly during the early days of *Raw*.

TOP **TEN** WORST THINGS ABOUT HAVING BELL'S PALSY

10 Not being able to wink when the need arises.

9 There goes my modeling career!

8 Constantly having to tell people, "No, I didn't have a stroke."

7 No party, but you still have a headache.

6 No whistling.

5 I lost my smile for real.

4 Can't listen to the Eagles as loudly as I used to.

3 Became a lousy kisser overnight.

2 Couldn't taste my wife's cooking.

1 It's an adventure to eat piping hot soup!

To Make Your Meal a "4-Star" Event!

SALADS AND SIDES

HAMMERLOCK

HAM SALAD

½ **cup lite salad dressing or reduced-fat mayonnaise**

½ **cup B&G emerald relish**

½ **tsp. sea salt**

¼ **tsp. coarse ground black pepper**

I **lb. cooked smoked boneless Black Forest ham, diced**

¼ **cup or medium onion minced**

I **tbsp. green pepper, seeded and diced**

½ **cup celery, finely chopped**

I *Stir* salad dressing or mayonnaise, relish, salt, and pepper in large bowl until well blended, adjust to taste.

2 Add ham, onion, pepper, and celery and toss until well coated. *Cover* and store in the refrigerator. Keeps three days.

SERVES 6

GRANNY ELSIE'S
SERVES 6
MACARONI

SALAD

I lb. elbow macaroni

¾ cup red bell pepper, seeded and diced

¾ cup green bell pepper, seeded and diced

I cup red onion, diced

½ cup celery, finely chopped

I cup Heinz Sweet Gherkin pickles, diced

I tbsp. sugar

I tsp. salt

½ tsp. pepper

2 tbsp. lite Miracle Whip

I *Cook* macaroni for about 10 minutes. Drain. Run cold water over macaroni until cool, drain well. In a large bowl mix peppers, onions, pickles. Add sugar, salt, and pepper, to taste, mix well. Add macaroni and salad dressing. Mix until well coated.

2 Refrigerate for several hours and *serve*.

LOIS'S FRESH CRANBERRY

SALAD

2 3-oz. package red raspberry Jell-O

1 cup hot water

½ cup cold water

1 small orange, peeled, diced, and seeded

½ cup pineapple, cubed and drained

1 cup whole berry cranberry sauce

¼ cup walnuts, chopped

Mix in a medium bowl Jell-O and waters. *Refrigerate* and chill until semifirm. Add orange, pineapple, cranberry sauce, and walnuts. Chill for 3 hours or until firm.

SERVES 4

LUCKY BLACK-EYED PEA SALAD

SERVES 5

1½ cups canned black-eyed peas, drained

¾ cup green pepper, seeded and diced

½ cup celery, diced

¾ cup red onion, chopped

¼ cup vegetable oil

¼ cup sugar

1½ tbsp. apple cider vinegar

1 clove garlic, minced

½ tsp. sea salt

½ tsp. coarse ground pepper

½ tsp. J.R.'s Hot Sauce

1 In a large bowl *combine* peas, pepper, celery, onion.

2 In a small bowl combine oil, sugar, vinegar, garlic, salt, pepper, and hot sauce. *Mix well.*

3 *Pour* the dressing over the beans, toss to coat, and refrigerate for 4 hours.

4 Can be *made* a day ahead.

SERVES 4 # JAN'S PASTA CAESAR SALAD

WITH TURKEY

1 6-oz. package penne pasta

1 lb. or 4 turkey breasts steaks, ½-inch thick

¾ cup Girard's Caesar Salad dressing, regular or lite

5 cups romaine lettuce, chopped

10 cherry tomatoes, seeded and halved

¼ cup fresh-grated Parmesan cheese

coarse ground pepper to taste

1 *Cook* pasta according to package directions. Drain and set aside.

2 On a gas grill, *preheat*, to medium.

3 For a charcoal: *grill* turkey on rack uncovered.

4 Over medium grill/coals cook for 15 minutes or until no longer pink. Turn and *baste* with ¼ cup of salad dressing halfway through grilling. Cool slightly and chop.

5 In a large bowl combine pasta, romaine, and tomatoes. Add remaining salad dressing and toss to coat. *Top* with chopped turkey and cheese and sprinkles of pepper if desired.

TEXAS FRITO SALAD

1 small head lettuce or packaged salad mix

¾ cup red onion, chopped

1 15-oz. can Sylvia's pinto beans, drained and rinsed

2 tomatoes, chopped

½ lb. shredded low-fat longhorn cheese

1 5-oz. package Fritos, bite sized

1 8-oz. bottle Catalina dressing

1 **Combine** in a large bowl lettuce, onion, beans, tomatoes, and cheese.

2 Add Fritos and dressing. **Serve**.

SERVES 8

HOT CHICKASHA CHICKEN SALAD

SERVES 4

I cup cooked rice (white or brown)

I cup cooked chicken, diced, or 9 oz. Louis Rich
   cooked chicken, diced

I cup celery, diced

I 10-oz. can Campbell's Cream of Chicken soup

¾ cup low-fat mayonnaise

½ cup water chestnuts, drained

¼ cup sliced almonds

3 tbsp. Vidala onion, chopped

I cup crushed Total cornflake crumbs

I tbsp. melted butter (optional)

1 *Preheat* oven to 350° F.

2 In an 8-inch-square baking dish *combine* rice, chicken, celery, soup, mayonnaise, water chestnuts, almonds, and onion. Top with cornflakes and drizzle with butter if desired.

3 *Bake* at 350° F for 45 minutes.

SAN ANTONIO GRILLED

6 flour tortillas

1 *Grill* tortillas over medium heat turning once until soft and lightly grill marked, about 1 minute on each side.

TORTILLAS

SERVES 3

TULSA TABOULEH

1½ cups cracked wheat

3 cups boiling water

1 8-oz. can of whole tomatoes, drained

½ cup cucumber, finely chopped

1 small onion, minced

½ cup red bell pepper, seeded and chopped

4 tbsp. fresh parsley, finely chopped

2 tbsp. fresh mint, finely chopped

4 tbsp. lemon juice

4 tbsp. olive oil

2 cloves garlic, minced

salt and pepper to taste

1   Place the cracked wheat in large bowl and cover with boiling water. Let stand for 30 minutes. *Drain* the wheat in a fine mesh strainer. Transfer the wheat to a large mixing bowl. Seed the tomatoes and dice. Add tomatoes, cucumber, pepper, onion, parsley, and mint to wheat mixture. Toss until mixed.

2   In a small bowl *mix* together lemon juice, oil, garlic, salt and pepper. Pour over the wheat, vegetables, and herbs and toss well to coat.

3   *Chill* in refrigerator for a few hours.

SERVES 4

HOME-STYLE

1 cup cornmeal

2 tbsp. flour

½ tsp. salt

1 tsp. baking powder

2 tbsp. butter

1 egg, beaten

¼ cup buttermilk, or sweetened condensed milk

1 Mix all ingredients. **Drop** tablespoons of batter onto medium skillet sprayed with Pam. Cook until golden.

HUSH PUPPIES

MY MAMA'S CORN BREAD

DRESSING

3 cups corn bread, crumbled

2½–3 cups biscuits, crumbled

1 medium onion, finely chopped

2 tsp. sage or to taste

1 tsp. salt

½ tsp. pepper

1 cup celery, chopped

2 cups chicken broth (Swanson's)

2 cubes chicken bouillon, crumbled

2 eggs, beaten

2 tbsp. butter

1 In large bowl mix corn bread and biscuits. Set aside. In a medium saucepan, add remaining ingredients and *cook* over medium heat for 10 minutes, or until onions are translucent. Add to corn bread mixture. Mix thoroughly, adjust seasonings to taste. Serve.

SERVES 6

J.R.'S TIP—*It's great stuffed in your favorite poultry!*

PICKLED  BEETS

- ¼ **cup onion, sliced**
- ¼ **cup sugar**
- ⅓ **cup white vinegar**
- ½ **tsp. cinnamon**
- ¼ **tsp. salt**
- ¼ **tsp. ground cloves**
- 1 **16-oz. can sliced beets, drained**

I In a medium saucepan *combine* onion, sugar, vinegar, cinnamon, salt, and cloves. Bring to a boil over a medium heat and cook for 5 minutes, stirring occasionally. Reduce heat to low and add beets. Simmer covered for 5 minutes. Cool. Then place pan in refrigerator for 6 to 8 hours. Drain before serving.

MAKES ½ QUART **DELI DILL PICKLES**

4 cups cucumbers, sliced ¼-to ½-inch thick

½ cup green bell pepper, sliced into slivers

½ cup celery, diced

½ cup onion, chopped into medium pieces

¾ tbsp. salt

1 cup sugar

½ cup vinegar

½ tsp. celery seed

½ tsp. mustard seed

1 *Mix* cucumber, pepper, celery, onion and salt in large bowl. Let stand for 30 minutes.

2 Meanwhile in a small saucepan over low heat *combine* sugar, vinegar, celery seed, and mustard seed until sugar is dissolved.

3 *Pour* over the cucumber mixture and toss several times.

4 Cool, then *seal* and refrigerate.

CRACKLIN'

1 13-oz. can of whole sweet potatoes or canned
   yams, drain and save liquid

1 6-oz. can crushed pineapple, drain and save liquid

½ cup honey

½ cup brown sugar

¼ cup white sugar

½ tsp. nutmeg

½ cup water

2 tbsp. flour

1 cup marshmallows

1 Preheat oven to 350° F. In medium saucepan, *pour* reserved liquid from the yams and the pineapple. Add crushed pineapple, honey, brown sugar, white sugar, and nutmeg. Bring to a boil on a medium heat. Slowly add water and flour, mix.

2 *Cook* until thickened slightly.

3 Arrange whole yams in a baking dish (8 x 8) and *pour* pineapple mixture over them and bake at 350° F for 30 minutes. Add marshmallows and cook for 5 minutes or until lightly browned.

CANDIED YAMS

SERVES 4 TO 6

BUSINESS-HAS-PICKED-UP

SERVES 4

BAKED BEANS

2 tbsp. butter or margarine

½ medium onion, chopped

⅓ cup bell pepper, chopped

1 10-oz. can Campbell's Pork & Beans

½ tsp. Wrights liquid smoke (hickory)

4 tbsp. ketchup

½ tsp. dry mustard

¼ cup light brown sugar

½ tsp. Worcestershire sauce

1 *Preheat* oven to 350° F. In medium saucepan, melt butter. Add onion and pepper and sauté until tender. In a large bowl mix beans, liquid smoke, ketchup, mustard, sugar, and Worcestershire sauce. Add in onion and peppers.

2 Pour into casserole dish and *bake* uncovered for 25 to 30 minutes.

THE **TEN** BIGGEST CHALLENGES OF BROADCASTING AT RINGSIDE

10 Too near the Spanish announcers' table (it's always a "target").

9 The King mentally going on an extended "puppy search."

8 Flying chairs and other dangerous "foreign objects."

7 You can't always scratch where you itch.

6 Fear of getting the hiccups.

5 No time for dinner.

4 Inebriated fans.

3 Extremely large men falling through our tables.

2 Gassy wrestlers.

1 No bathroom breaks.

GRANNY MAE'S
COLLARD

GREENS

2 lbs. fresh collards

5 tbsp. corn oil

1 cup sliced pork, or 3 oz. bacon

1½ cups water

4 tsp. sugar

1 tsp. sea salt

1 Wash the collards two or three times and make sure the dirt has been removed. Coarsely *chop* the greens.

2 Heat the oil in a large pot and then add the meat and cook until partly browned on all sides, about 5 minutes. Add the water and bring to a boil. Reduce the heat and *simmer* for 15 minutes. Add collards to pot. Add the sugar and salt. Cover and cook on medium heat about 30 minutes.

3 *Serve* using a slotted spoon.

SERVES 8-10

WESTVILLE YELLOW JACKET

PINTO BEANS

½ lb. dried pinto beans

water to cover

1 lb. smoked ham hock

½ cup chopped onion

1-1½ tsp. salt

½ tsp. coarse ground black pepper

½ tsp. sugar

1 small clove garlic, crushed

water to cover

1   In a large bowl *soak* the beans covered in water overnight. Drain well.

2   In large saucepot combine all ingredients. Cover with water and bring to a boil on medium-high heat then reduce heat to low so it is simmering. Cover and *cook* until the beans are tender, approximately 45 minutes.

3   *Adjust* seasonings and serve hot.

J.R.'S TIP—*Great with corn bread.*

OKLAHOMA OKRA

PATTIES

SERVES 8

4 cups fresh or frozen (thawed) okra

½ cup olive oil

3 eggs

1 medium onion, chopped

½ cup water

1½ tsp. salt or to taste

pepper to taste

1 cup flour

1 Wash the okra and drain. *Remove* stems and cut into ½-inch slices. Salt okra. Blend eggs, onion, and water with salt and pepper. Add okra, then add flour and mix well.

2 *Heat* oil in large skillet over medium-low heat. Put okra slices in heated oil. Turn okra while cooking until crispy and lightly browned, about 8–10 minutes. Drain on paper towels.

3 Green tomatoes may also be prepared this way, *chopped* not sliced.

GRILLED HARVEST

6 corn ears (husk and silk removed)

Pam cooking spray

butter, softened

salt and pepper

1 Take corn and *spray* lightly with Pam then add salt and pepper to taste. Grill about 5–8 minutes, turning while cooking. Grill until light grill marks appear.

CORN

MAKES 6

J.R.'S TIP—*For a smoky flavor combine ½ tablespoon of chili powder mixed with juice of ¼ lemon and ¼ cup melted butter. Apply to corn instead of Pam mix.*

SMASHED DOWN POTATOES

4 Idaho potatoes, peeled and cubed

4 tbsp. butter (½ stick) room temperature

½ cup milk, heated until warm

¼ cup reduced-fat sour cream

salt and coarse ground pepper to taste

1 Place potatoes in medium pan. Cover with water and bring to a boil. Reduce heat and cook for 20–30 minutes. *Drain* potatoes and return to saucepan. Add remaining ingredients and blend until smooth.

2 *Serve* immediately.

SERVES 4

SERVES 2 # ROASTED

REDS

12 small red potatoes about 2-in. thick, rinsed and scrubbed

nonstick spray

1 tbsp. olive oil

1 tbsp. paprika

¼ tsp. cayenne pepper

½ tbsp. garlic powder

1 tsp. sea salt

1 Prepare gas grill or a charcoal grill for direct cooking over medium heat. *Spray* the grill rack. In a large pot boil water. Add potatoes and cook about 5 minutes until easily pierced with a knife but not completely tender. Drain and pat dry. Place potatoes in a large bowl and coat with oil.

2 In a small bowl, *mix* paprika, cayenne pepper, garlic powder, salt. Add to potatoes and toss until well coated.

3 Grill potatoes directly over medium-high heat, *turning* until browned and tender, approximately 10–15 minutes.

4 *Serve* hot.

J.R.'S TIP—*May be doubled.*

J.R.'S TOP TEN THINGS YOU PROBABLY DON'T KNOW ABOUT JERRY "THE KING" LAWLER

10 Eats junk food and never gains weight.

9 Does not own a jacket and refuses to wear one no matter how cold it is.

8 Works very hard to achieve his "Superman" hair curl.

7 "Doodles" on his *Raw* TV format sheet during every broadcast, no matter how good or bad the show is. (The King is an awesome artist.)

6 Almost always forgets his crown before every *Raw*.

5 Turns down dates from beautiful women *over the age of thirty.*

4 Believes the Cleveland Browns will win the Super Bowl, every year.

3 Believes the Cleveland Indians will win the World Series, every year.

2 Is as big a shopping mall–aholic as any female. Goes to a mall in virtually every city we produce *Raw*.

1 Shaves his body hair. (**OK**, so not everybody knew that, but now they do. And while doing it he once almost cut off his nipple!)

I have worked with many talented broadcast partners, but Jerry Lawler is my favorite. King's jacket is from the "Sir Elton John Collection."

TAHLEQUAH
TORTILLA
SERVES 4 – 6
SOUP

1 15-oz. can of tomatos with green chiles

1 medium onion, chopped

1 1.25-oz. pkg. taco seasoning mix

2 qts. Swanson's chicken broth

2 tbsp. cilantro

2 tsp. ground cumin

1 cup cooked shredded chicken

8½ oz. Tostitos reduced-fat tortilla chips, slightly crushed

cheddar cheese

green onions, chopped

1   In a large pot bring tomatos, onion, taco seasoning, broth, cilantro, cumin, and chicken to a boil. *Reduce* heat and simmer for 30 minutes. Garnish with chips, cheese, and onion. Serve immediately.

PAPA'S POTATO

4 medium white potatoes, peeled and chopped

2 tbsp. butter

1 small onion, sliced

3 cups milk

⅛ tsp. cayenne pepper

½ tsp. salt

⅛ tsp. celery salt

black pepper to taste

2 tbsp. chopped parsley

1 Place potatoes in pot with enough water to cover them. Bring to a *boil* for 15 minutes.

2 Meanwhile melt the butter in medium skillet over medium-low heat. Add onion and cook uncovered for 5 minutes or until soft. Set aside. When potatoes are done, *drain* in a colander. Return potatoes to pot. Mash them while they are warm off the stove. Add onion and mix. Stir in milk, cayenne pepper, salt, celery salt, and black pepper. Cook over medium heat stirring frequently, about 10 minutes.

3 *Garnish* with parsley.

PILLMAN'S
PASSION

I was living in Dallas in 1989 working for WCW when I got word that Kim Wood, the strength coach for the NFL's Cincinnati Bengals, was trying to get a hold of me. Being one of the world's biggest football fans, I was curious as to why, so I returned the call.

Kim, a great fan of our business and a wonderful man, was suggesting that WCW hire a young wrestler named **Brian Pillman** who had played for a time for the Bengals and who was currently wrestling in the Calgary territory. I had never met Brian, nor had I ever seen him perform, but I knew if he was trained by Stu Hart and family, that he couldn't be bad, and certainly if he played in the NFL he had to be athletic. Kim said Brian was one of the toughest and most passionate athletes he had ever seen in his long career in the NFL.

One phone call lead to another, and finally I got Brian hired in **WCW** sometime in the spring of '89. That's when our friendship began, and it continued until the day he died, October 6, 1997, at the age of thirty-five, while on the talent roster that I managed for WWE.

Officially, Brian died of heart failure, but his death was much more complex for me personally. I loved Brian like a little brother. I worried about him constantly and spent hours on the telephone talking to him about his seemingly endless list of family problems, personal problems, and professional challenges. Brian wanted, perhaps more than anyone I have ever known, to be one of the all-time-great in-ring performers in the history of our business.

Would it be challenging? Of course, but you have to remember this was a guy who was born with throat cancer and had an incredible thirty-one operations on his throat by the time he was three years old! Challenges? Who are you kidding? But a Humvee accident that shattered his ankle also shattered those dreams of my friend Brian, who refused to accept that verdict.

Brian Pillman, whose untimely death had a profound effect on me, had the ability to become one of the best color analysts of all time.

Brian became my broadcast partner, and we were grooming him to become the next Jesse "the Body" Ventura. There is no doubt in my mind that Brian Pillman would have eventually become the greatest villain commentator in the history of the business, had he lived. We talked about his career moving on, from the ring to the broadcast booth, but I could tell his heart was broken. This was one situation he found himself in that even Brian knew he could not get out of. And I did not know how to help him. We talked almost daily about the hand that was dealt him and we cried together over his frustration, many times stopping our voice-overs and going for a walk behind the **WWE TV** studios in Stamford, Connecticut. But I never could make him see that he had so much to live for and to count his blessings, because this new role was tailor-made for him.

There is not a week of my life that goes by that I do not think of Brian Pillman in some way. Recently looking through a box of mementos of my career, I found an autographed photo Brian sent to me in 1989 of **Bengal Stanley Wilson**, a former Oklahoma Sooner and Cincinnati running back who missed the Bengals Super Bowl game many years ago, allegedly because of drugs.

How ironic. Drugs were Stanley's demons, and they beat him on that day. Brian's demon was his uncontrollable passion, which left him with a broken heart.

IT'S TIME,
IT'S TIME,
IT'S TOGA TIME!!

WrestleMania IX in Las Vegas, April 4, 1993, was my first live broadcast for WWE after I departed Ted Turner's WCW, and it was the first and last time in my life I ever wore a toga! The event was held outdoors at Caesar's Palace and had a Roman theme, thus everyone broadcasting the event wore attire befitting the venue. For some reason, people have thought for years that I had a problem wearing this unique clothing for my debut at the "show," but that was not the case at all. I had worked almost twenty years in the business at that point with the express purpose of making it to the top level of our profession someday. I probably would have worn a Speedo bathing suit with cowboy boots if **Vince McMahon** had asked me to, just to be a part of the biggest sports entertainment extravaganza in the industry. (Thank goodness, he didn't!)

Before the show, Vince came to me in private and asked me if I had a problem wearing the toga and that if I did, I could attend the event, observe

Bobby "the Brain" Heenan wanted me to go "commando" (meaning no underwear), but I thought better of it.

backstage, and debut the next month at the *King of the Ring.* Again, there was no way I was going to let this opportunity pass me by. After being unceremoniously dumped by the mental pygmies in Atlanta, I still had two and a half years left on my contract. I felt I had something to prove to Turner, the fans, and, most importantly, to myself. I had come into the business as a fan and worked damn hard to become a competent broadcaster, and I think I needed to get back in the saddle sooner than later and do what I loved doing— calling wrestling matches for the pure love of the game.

Vince wanted to remain backstage for that huge production complete with tons of extras and animals, including elephants! Gorilla Monsoon would have normally got the nod to do the play by play, but he was very ill that day and only made a cameo at the very top of the show. I broadcast the show with the incomparable **Bobby "the Brain"** Heenan and Randy "Macho Man" Savage from ringside. It was the fateful afternoon Undertaker wrestled one of the more athletically untalented men to ever grace a ring, El Gigante, and the triumphant return of Hulk Hogan, who would win the title from Yokozuna, just a few minutes after Yoko defeated **Bret "the Hitman" Hart,** because Yoko's manager, Mr. Fuji, threw "salt" in the eyes of the Hitman, which enabled the HUGE challenger to become champion. Hogan would remain champion until the next month's *King of the Ring* PPV, where he would lose back the title to the massive Samoan in the usual "match filled with controversy," and then leave the company for "creative reasons."

But back to the toga. The Brain suggested I go **"commando"** under the toga, i.e., wear no underwear so as to truly experience the "feel" of the garment. In the midst of two, or maybe four, Crown Royals and water the night before the event, I actually considered doing it, but I soon sobered—err—smartened up, and opted to wear gym shorts under the infamous toga. For some reason, I felt like the "Wease" just might be setting me up for a classic rib, perhaps even orchestrated by **Mr. McMahon** himself, and I thought I better cover my bases, so to speak. All in all, *WrestleMania IX* was a day I will never forget and will always remember fondly, toga and all!

the biggest sports

entertainment

extravaganza

in the industry

OWEN, THE BULLDOG, AND THE STATUE

In the old days of the Calgary wrestling territory, owned and operated by Stu Hart and his unique family, the trips throughout Alberta in the wintertime are the foundation for some of the legendary tall tales in our business. The wrestlers oftentimes traveled in two old vans, the "good guys" in one and the "villains" in another. One very cold winter night, with the defroster not working on one of the vans, the boys decided to pull into a small town to clean the windshield. This was about two hours after a live event in some obscure locale, and the **British Bulldog Davey Boy Smith**, as the legend goes, had fallen into a deep sleep, perhaps aided by too much strong Canadian ale. The van stopped in a town square where a large statue some ten feet high of a local hero was the primary focal point. Owen's mind raced with the thought of a great rib he planned to play on his then brother-in-law, the British Bulldog. As the younger wrestlers braved the elements and cleaned the ice from the windshield, Owen woke Davey up from his very sound sleep. "Davey, there is a guy standing out here who says wrestling is fake and he says he can whip anybody in our van! You can't let him talk to us that way!"

The powerful Bulldog bolts out of the van ready for war! Davey marches right up to the statue and begins cutting a scathing promo, or as we say in Oklahoma, how the cow ate the cabbage, challenging the stoic concrete figure to fight! Allegedly, this went on for about two or three minutes until everyone was laughing hysterically and **Davey** finally realized he was challenging a statue to fight him! Davey wanted to kill Owen until he started laughing, too, and all was forgotten at least for the balance of that infamous road trip. There is no doubt in my mind that somewhere down the road Davey probably got even with Owen, but no one ever truly got the upper hand on the youngest Hart when it came to ribbing.

Two of the greatest "ribbers" ever in the business, Davey Boy Smith and Owen Hart. Both of these great athletes have moved on to wrestling in Heaven, but neither will ever be forgotten.

Main dishes
and entrées

And now, Ladies and Gentlemen,

J.R. presents . . .

THE MAIN EVENT!

J.R.'S BBQ CHICKEN

**I 3-to-4-lb. chicken cut into eighths or 8 skinless
chicken thighs**

3 cups J.R.'s BBQ Sauce

salt and pepper to taste

I *Rinse* the chicken under cold water and pat dry with paper towels. Place in bowl and pour in 1 cup sauce. Cover and marinate in refrigerator for 3 hours or more.

2 Heat the grill to medium heat. Place chicken on medium heat on grill and cook for 10 minutes, then *turn* and cook 10 more minutes. Discard any remaining marinade. Pour 1 cup of sauce in small bowl and baste the chicken with it. Grill until juices run clear and internal temperature is 180° F.

3 Heat remaining cup of sauce and *serve* on the side.

4 *Add* salt and pepper to taste.

S E R V E S   4

LIZZIE'S HEALTHY

CHICKEN

1 cup pineapple juice

½ cup honey

1 tbsp. garlic, jar or fresh minced

6 tbsp. Worcestershire sauce

2 tsp. ground ginger

2 tsp. sea salt

8 chicken thighs or breasts (skinless)

1 In medium saucepan *mix* together pineapple juice, honey, garlic, Worcestershire, ginger, salt. Over a medium flame, bring to boil and reduce heat and simmer 10 minutes. Let cool. Reserve ¼ cup of marinade. Rinse and pat dry chicken and place in large bowl. Pour the rest of marinade over chicken, cover and refrigerate for 6 to 7 hours. Drain and discard marinade.

2 *Heat* grill to medium.

3 Grill on medium hot coals. Cover and grill until chicken is tender and no longer pink. *Brush* with remaining marinade while cooking.

SERVES 4

"IN THIS CORNER . . ."
THE KING
VERSUS PAUL E.

These two men have a great deal in common. Really! They are both huge students of the game and have been considered to be among the best ever in their respective careers in the business BEFORE they started broadcasting. The King, as a wrestler in his hometown of Memphis for decades, and **Paul Heyman,** as a wisecracking, usually abrasive New Yorker, who's been a wrestling manager in a variety of "territories."

The King is a little easier for me to work with because he is so laid-back, rarely gets rattled, and you always know what to expect working with him. He is normally lighthearted, unless he is "between lady friends," and has a natural, comedic wit. Low maintenance fits **Jerry "the King" Lawler.** I would like to think we complement each other very well, and the King is the most comfortable partner I have ever broadcast with to date.

Paul Heyman, formerly known as **Paul E. Dangerously,** is a true student of the game as well and has been a huge fan of the business his entire life. He is the only child of a very successful personal injury attorney from Scarsdale, New York. Paul is hyper, oftentimes over the top, and was the one partner I have had over the years that truly kept me on the edge of my seat and completely on my toes every moment of every broadcast. I was never quite sure what he was going to say or in what direction he was going to head. Not that any of that is a bad thing. I will say working with Paul over the years has probably contributed to my blood pressure issues, but then again, I could be wrong about that. With my style being just a little bit over the top at times (okay, most of the time), and being very emotional about our product, the combination of the two of us was too much for some folks' tastes. But as an antagonist, Paul was superb because, as I told him five minutes after we first met, his character is so easy to dislike. **King or Heyman?** It's like asking beef or pork? They're both very good when properly prepared with the right side dishes.

J.R.'S BEST BROILED SALMON WITH CILANTRO TOMATO CAPER

SALSA

CILANTRO TOMATO CAPER SALSA

1 tbsp. olive oil

6 plum tomatoes, seeded and chopped

1 tbsp. capers

½ cup shallots, chopped

⅓ cup cilantro, chopped

salt and coarse ground pepper to taste

½ tsp. lemon juice

3 1½-inch salmon fillets

lemon juice to taste

1 tbsp. olive oil

salt

pepper

SERVES 6

1 Mix oil, tomatoes, capers, onion, cilantro, salt and pepper, and lemon juice in a bowl and *blend* well, adjusting seasonings. Cover and place in refrigerator for 3 hours, stirring occasionally.

2 *Heat* oven to broil.

3 Rinse salmon fillets and pat dry. Place on aluminum foil and brush with oil to coat fish completely. *Sprinkle* with salt and pepper and lemon. Broil in oven until fish is browned and thickest part is cooked through, about 15–20 minutes. Check to see if fish flakes easily when tested with a fork.

4 Top with tomato caper salsa and serve hot.

J.R.'S TIP—*Works great on a grill too!*

SERVES 4 # FIREHOUSE ROASTED MESQUITE CHICKEN

RUB

1 tbsp. paprika

1 tbsp. light brown sugar

½ tbsp. chili powder

2 drops liquid smoke, mesquite

½ tbsp. sea salt

½ tbsp. coarse ground pepper

1 tsp. garlic, minced

1½ tsp. onion powder

½ tsp. cumin

1 3½-to-4-lbs. whole chicken

mesquite chips soaked in water for 30 minutes

1 *Heat* grill to medium.

2 Combine paprika, brown sugar, chili powder, liquid smoke, sea salt, pepper, garlic, onion powder, and cumin in a small bowl and set aside. Remove and discard neck and giblets from the chicken. *Rinse* the chicken inside and out and pat dry. Cut the chicken in half and carefully remove the backbones. Coat chicken halves with rub, place in bowl, and cover with plastic wrap. Place in refrigerator for 3 hours. Follow the grill's instructions for using wood chips. Grill the chicken halves, skin side up, over indirect medium heat until the juices run clear, about 1¼ hour.

J.R.'S BABY BACK RIBS

RUB

½ tsp. onion powder

½ tsp. garlic powder

salt and pepper to taste

5 drops of liquid smoke

1 *Combine* all ingredients in a bowl.

2 1-to-1½-lb. racks of baby back ribs

liquid smoke, hickory or mesquite

salt and pepper to taste

1 tsp. garlic powder, to taste

rub

J.R.'s BBQ Sauce

Williams Smoker Bag

2 Rinse and pat dry ribs. Rub a few drops of liquid smoke into meat. Rub salt and pepper and garlic powder and *rub* into meat. Then coat generously with BBQ sauce. Let stand in refrigerator for 3 hours. Place racks in Williams Smoker Bag and grill or bake as directed on package.

SERVES 3 - 4

SIMPLE SMOKED

SERVES 2

1 lb. cut-up chicken pieces

½–1 tsp. Sylvia's chicken rub or to taste

1 Williams poultry smoker bag

1 *Rinse* and pat dry chicken. Rub Sylvia's chicken rub over chicken.

2 Place chicken in smoker bag. *Seal* and cook as directed on package.

CHICKEN

TEX-MEX TEQUILA

RIBS

SERVES 4

2½ lbs. pork spare ribs

sea salt

black pepper, coarsely ground

¾ cup olive oil

¾ cup fresh lime juice

⅓ cup tequila

¼ cup onion, chopped

2 tsp. garlic, minced

1 small jalapeño, seeded and chopped

salt and pepper to taste

1 *Wash* and pat dry ribs. Place in a glass baking dish. Season with sea salt and pepper. In a small bowl place olive oil, lime juice, tequila, onion, garlic, jalapeño, salt and pepper. Mix well. Reserve ¼ of the mix for basting. Pour remainder over ribs, coating all sides.

2 Cover and *refrigerate* for 6 to 8 hours.

3 *Preheat* grill to low.

4 Place ribs meat side down on grill and cook, *basting* every 20 minutes. Cook for 1½–2 hours or until cooked throughout and ribs are tender.

J.R.'S TIP—*When handling hot peppers, use rubber or plastic gloves to protect your hands, and avoid touching your face.*

BOY HOWDY BEEF-VEGETABLE STEW

2 tbsp. olive oil

5 slices bacon, cut into 1-inch pieces

1¾ lbs. boneless beef tenderloin, cut into 1-inch cubes

coarse ground pepper

10–12 baby carrots

4 parsnips, peeled and cut into 3-inch lengths

8 leeks, white parts only, rinsed very well, sliced

2 tbsp. sugar

1½ cups beef broth

1½ cups red wine or burgundy

2 tbsp. unsalted butter

2 tbsp. red currant jelly

2 tsp. thyme

6–8 small new red potatoes, cut in half

6–8 garlic cloves, minced

5 ripe plum tomatoes, seeded and chopped

⅓ cup Italian parsley, chopped

cooked egg noodles

SERVES 8

1 *Preheat* oven to 350° F.

2 Heat oil in a large pan. Add bacon and cook over medium heat for 5 minutes. *Transfer* bacon to large casserole dish. Brown the beef in same skillet over medium-high heat. Season with pepper. Add beef to casserole dish.

3 In the skillet, *sauté* carrots, parsnips, leeks, and sugar. Cook for 7 minutes. Remove vegetables and set aside in medium bowl.

4 Add broth, red wine, butter, jelly, and thyme to skillet and bring to boil and cook for about 2 minutes. *Pour* over meat in casserole dish. Add potatoes and garlic to casserole and bake for 45 minutes. Remove casserole and add vegetables and parsley, stir. Bake uncovered for another 45 minutes.

5 *Serve* with egg noodles.

PILEDRIVER

PORK CHOPS

6 ½-inch thick boneless pork chops

2 tbsp. light brown sugar

2 tbsp. olive oil

2 tbsp. orange juice

1 tbsp. apple cider vinegar

2 tsp. chili powder

1 tsp. cumin

1 tsp. oregano

½ tsp. salt

¼ tsp. cinnamon

½ tsp. red pepper

3 cloves garlic, minced

3 tbsp. dried cilantro, chopped

1 *Rinse* and pat dry chops. Place the chops in a shallow glass dish or large bowl. Set aside.

2 In a small bowl combine all the ingredients and mix well. *Pour* over chops and cover and marinate in the refrigerator for several hours. Drain chops and discard marinade.

3 Heat grill to medium. *Grill* chops on the rack of an uncovered charcoal grill over medium heat for 10 minutes or until desired doneness, turning during cooking. Juices should run clear.

4 For gas grill, *cover* and cook as above.

SERVES 6

SOONER NATION

4 ¾-lb. ½-inch thick New York strip steaks

2 tbsp. Head Country BBQ seasoning

3 drops hickory smoke

salt and coarse ground pepper to taste

1   *Heat* grill to high.

2   Rinse and pat dry steaks. *Rub* BBQ seasoning into steaks along with salt, pepper, and smoke. Grill over direct high heat until the internal temperature reaches 145° F for medium-rare, about 8–10 minutes, turning once halfway through grilling time. Cook until desired to your liking.

J.R.'S TIP—*Not in Ponca City? You can get Head Country BBQ seasoning by calling (888) 762-1227 or visiting www.headcountry.com.*

STRIP STEAK

SERVES 4

E-Z GLAZED

HAM STEAK

1 1½-to-2-lb. fully cooked ham slice, cut 1-inch thick

2 tbsp. Boar's Head brown sugar and spice ham glaze

1   Place ham slice in a pan on medium-low heat. *Cook* for a total of 5–10 minutes on each side. Turn frequently. Do not burn, so you may need to reduce the heat. Brush 1 tbsp. glaze on the ham and cook for 5–10 minutes. Repeat on the other side. Serve.

ON A GRILL

1   Heat grill to medium. For a gas grill *preheat* grill and reduce to medium.

2   *Brush* both sides of ham with 1 tbsp. ham glaze.

3   To prevent ham from curling, make shallow *cuts* around the edge at 1-inch intervals.

4   *Grill* ham on the rack of an uncovered grill directly over medium coals for 10–15 minutes.

5   *Turn* ham and grill for 5 minutes more or until desired doneness.

SERVES 2

SLOBBERKNOCKER

2 6-oz. salmon steaks

3 tbsp. honey

1 tsp. Country-style Dijon mustard (Grey Poupon)

1 Heat grill to medium. *Rinse* and pat dry salmon. Set pieces on aluminum foil. In a small bowl, mix honey and mustard well.

2 *Set* salmon on foil onto grill (or broil in oven on rack on middle level of oven).

3 *Spread* honey mix on salmon and grill (or broil) away from direct heat. Make sure honey mustard doesn't burn.

4 Cook for about 15–20 minutes (*add* 5 minutes more for broiler) or until thick part of flesh is cooked through.

SALMON

SERVES 2

SERVES 4

SUCCULENT GRILLED

LOBSTER TAILS

4 frozen 5-to-6-oz. rock lobster tails

¼ cup butter, melted

1 tsp. lemon juice

dash of ground ginger

pinch of chili powder

1 *Heat* grill to high, then reduce to medium high.

2 Thaw lobster tails. *Cut* off the thin undershell membrane with scissors or sharp knife. Insert long skewers lengthwise between the shell and meat to prevent curling.

3 Combine butter, lemon juice, ginger, chili powder in a small bowl. *Brush* over lobster meat.

4 With meat side up, *grill* lobster tails over hot coals about 7 minutes. Brush with sauce and turn shell side up. Grill 6–8 minutes more or until meat is opaque and has no transparency. Discard sauce and serve immediately.

J.R.'S GREAT GRILLED

TROUT

4 10-to-12-oz. fresh trout fillets

⅓ cup all-purpose flour

½ tsp. salt

⅛ tsp. pepper

dash of cayenne pepper

¼ tsp. paprika

¼ cup butter or margarine melted

1 *Heat* grill to high.

2 In a medium bowl combine flour, salt, pepper, cayenne, and paprika. Rinse and pat dry fish then dip fish in seasoned flour, thoroughly coating it. Place coated fish in a wire grill basket or hinged basket. *Grill* fish over hot coals about 10 minutes.

3 Turn fish and baste with melted butter. Grill 10 minutes more and continue *basting* with butter. Discard butter.

4 *Cook* until fish flakes easily when tested with a fork.

TEN THINGS TO *NEVER* SAY TO VINCE MCMAHON

10 "You look tired."

9 "It doesn't matter what the fans think."

8 "Want a french fry?"

7 "Got a light?" or "Mind if I smoke?"

6 "Vince, you *can't* do that."

5 "Okay if I sneeze?"

4 "You're putting *ketchup* on that steak?!"

3 "There is NO WAY you can lift that!"

2 "That will *never* work, Vince."

1 "There is *NO WAY* that even *YOU* can get that guy over."

**Heart-*Healthy*
Turkey Chili**

(page 191)

**SmackDown!
*S'Mores***

(page 221)

Jan Ross's *Chicken* Cacciatore

(page 200)

Sooner Nation *Strip Steak* (page 173)

Banana Split *Shake* (page 248)

Old-Fashioned Southern *Sun Tea* (page 247)

Slobberknocker **Salmon** (page 175)
and Lois's Fresh Cranberry *Salad* (page 126)

J.R.'s Baby Back *Ribs* (page 167)
and *Grilled* Harvest Corn (page 143)

WrestleMania **Burger!** (page 60)

**J.R.'s
Creamy
Coconut
Cream *Pie***

(page 237)

**Jan's Fresh
Blueberry
*Tart***

(page 230)

Bad Ass Chilean *Sea Bass* (page 181)

FLAME-BROILED

TUNA STEAKS

4 6-to-8-oz. fresh tuna steaks

3 tbsp. soy sauce

1 tbsp. Worcestershire sauce

½ tsp. Dijon-style mustard

1 tsp. sugar or honey

1 tbsp. vegetable oil

lemon wedges for garnish

1 *Heat* grill to medium.

2 Rinse and pat dry tuna steaks and place in shallow dish. Mix the soy sauce, Worcestershire, mustard, sugar, and oil in a small bowl then pour over the tuna. *Turn* them gently over and make sure they are well coated with the marinade. Cover and refrigerate for 1 hour. Broil the tuna over hot coals, turning once for 10–15 minutes. Grill to desired doneness.

SERVES 4

COUNTRY CORNISH HENS

SERVES 4

2 1¼-lb. fresh Cornish game hens

⅓ cup fresh basil leaves

⅓ cup fresh parsley

¼ cup olive oil

2 tbsp. lemon juice

½ tbsp. Dijon-style mustard

1 tsp. fresh rosemary

1 clove garlic, minced

¼ tsp. salt

¼ tsp. pepper

1 Rinse and pat dry hens. *Cut* into halves lengthwise. Place hens in a deep nonmetallic bowl.

2 In blender, *combine* basil, parsley, oil, lemon juice, mustard, rosemary, and garlic. Blend until almost smooth. Pour ½ mixture over hens, cover and refrigerate for 4 to 6 hours. Refrigerate the remaining mixture separately. Heat grill to medium hot.

3 *Drain* hens, discarding marinade. Arrange medium-hot coals around a drip pan. Place hens skin side up on medium heat on grill rack. Cover and grill for 45–50 minutes or until no longer pink near bone.

4 Gas grill: cover and *cook* as above on medium heat.

5 *Serve* with remaining herb mixture.

BAD ASS CHILEAN

SEA BASS

2 tbsp. flour

salt and pepper to taste

pinch of cayenne pepper, or to taste

2 6-to-8-oz. Chilean sea bass fillets

2 tbsp. olive oil

I *Combine* in a bowl flour, salt, pepper, and cayenne. Place fillets in flour mixture and lightly coat both sides. Heat oil in a medium skillet over medium heat. Sauté for 4–5 minutes on each side, until golden brown and cooked throughout.

SERVES 2

"WE PREFER YOU CALL HIM GOVERNOR VENTURA"

Over the years, I have developed a unique relationship with the former Minnesota governor Jesse Ventura. Jesse "the Body" Ventura was the first controversial TV commentator to gain national prominence in our business when he came on the scene in the early 1980s. As he is today in politics, and in every aspect of his life, Jesse is outspoken and opinionated. He is very bright with an extensive street-smart education and in my opinion did an excellent job for the state of Minnesota as their governor. We broadcasted a few XFL football games together on NBC during the controversial league's one season. I have grown to respect **Jesse** for his accomplishments away from wrestling, and I have reevaluated his contributions to our business as well. But it has not always been that way.

In the past Jesse and I butted heads somewhat, when he signed on with Turner's WCW and became my regular broadcast partner on the SuperStation and PPV broadcasts. You see, I like to prepare, and Jesse didn't. I made copious notes for every broadcast and wanted to go over them in depth with my then-partner, but he would rather talk about the Navy SEALS, "Ah-nold," or tell **Mad Dog Vachon** stories. He also loved to argue politics.

Looking back on it I probably should have loosened up a little and relaxed and simply accepted that Jesse is "Jesse" and he will either get the job done, or he won't. Don't stress over what you can't control I suppose, but in those days I was a little higher-strung, to say the least. I have dozens of Ventura stories.

Let me tell you two quick ones.

On July 20, 1992, we were going to broadcast one of our first PPV's together, and it was in Mobile, Alabama, called *Blast at the Beach*. The night before the event we decided to get together in my room to go over the show, but I don't think we ever did. One story, from each of us, lead to another, in what became a "smoked-filled room." It was an interesting night to say the least.

A few years later, when **"the Body"** and I hooked up for our short stint together in the XFL, I had put all—okay most—of my ego-based in-

The former governor of Minnesota, Jesse "the Body" Ventura, and yours truly, during the live *Clash of The Champions XX*, broadcast on Sept. 2, 1992.

securities behind me and was excited for the opportunity to work with Jesse again on a unique stage, professional football. He always traveled with quite an entourage that oftentimes included the obligatory security force, his lawyer from time to time, his LA–based agent, **Barry Bloom,** and his personal football producer, who helped him prepare for the games on the chartered Lear jet flight from Minneapolis to our game site. Before we met for the first time after my assignment to the "A" game on NBC in week two of the XFL season, I casually mentioned to someone in his group that I was excited to have the opportunity to work with Jesse again and that "the Body" always kept me on my toes, etc., etc., etc. I was quickly informed, in no uncertain terms, that THEY preferred that I call him "Governor Ventura" in private, but that I could call him Jesse on television. I immediately thought of where they could place their bureaucratic lips in relation to my sizable Oklahoma backside, but I played along and said, "Sure, no problem."

As I walked into my broadcast partner's suite, I said, "Hello, **Governor Ventura,**" and Jesse, smoking a big cigar, looked at me like I was crazy for being so formal with him. I don't think his aides knew that Ventura loved being "the Body," perhaps more than being the "Governor."

OVEN-ROASTED

1 10-to-12-lb. fresh turkey

4 tbsp. butter

1 tbsp. sage

1 tbsp. poultry seasoning

½ tsp. salt, or to taste

½ tsp. pepper, or to taste

½ garlic powder

1 cup chicken broth

3 medium potatoes, quartered

3 parsnips, halved and cut into 3-inch pieces

2 stalks celery, cut into 2-inch pieces

1 large onion, quartered

5 sprigs parsley

4 carrots cut into 3-inch pieces

⅓ cup white wine

Pam cooking spray

TURKEY

1 *Preheat* oven to 325° F.

2 Remove the neck and giblets and rinse the turkey well. Pat dry. Place the bird in a large roasting pan and *rub* the bird well, inside and out, with the butter, sage, poultry seasoning, salt, pepper, and garlic powder. Rub butter under the skin as well. Spray with Pam. If unstuffed, place vegetables inside and around the turkey; if stuffed, place vegetables in pan. Then pour chicken broth and wine around the turkey. Cover and cook turkey as directed on package, basting every 20 minutes. Cook about ½ hour per pound or until thermometer reads 180° F (in the thickest part of the bird) and it's browned, approximately 3 hours for a 10-pound turkey.

SERVES 4–6 # SANTA MARIA FLANK STEAK

FAJITAS

½ cup vegetable oil

1 yellow onion, chopped

1 jalapeño chili, seeded and chopped, to taste

2 cloves garlic, chopped

1 tbsp. fresh oregano, chopped

1 tsp. cumin

1 tbsp. chili powder

3 tbsp. fresh cilantro, chopped

2 tbsp. lime juice

1½ tsp. salt

pepper to taste

1 2½-lb. flank steak

1   In a small bowl, *mix* together the oil, onion, jalapeño chili, garlic, oregano, cumin, chili powder, cilantro, lime juice, salt and pepper. Cut rinsed steak a few times across the grain and then cut into 4 pieces. Put the steak in a large Ziploc plastic bag and pour marinade over it. Refrigerate for 3–5 hours or overnight, turning occasionally. Remove the steak from the marinade.

2   *Prepare* the grill (charcoal or gas) for direct grilling over medium-high heat.

3   Grill the steak for 5–8 minutes on each side, *turning* once or until medium or medium-rare. May be served with grilled tortillas, salsa, pico de gallo, and guacamole.

FIRE-ROASTED

VEGETABLE

1 red bell pepper, seeded and cut into wedges

1 yellow bell pepper, seeded and cut into wedges

1 green bell pepper, seeded and cut into wedges

1 yellow onion or red onion, quartered

10 cherry tomatoes

4 ozs. mushrooms

SEASONED OIL

6 tbsp. olive oil

1 clove garlic crushed or 1 tsp. garlic powder

1 tsp. Emeril's vegetable dust or 1 tsp. seasoned salt

¼ tsp. pepper

1 Heat grill to medium hot. *Thread* the peppers, onions, tomatoes, and mushrooms on skewers alternating colors of peppers. Make seasoned oil by mixing together all remaining ingredients until well blended. Brush the mixture over the kebobs until well coated.

2 Broil the kebobs over medium-hot coals for 10–15 minutes, brushing with oil and *turning* the kebobs frequently.

SERVES 6

CHARBROILED STEAK AND SHRIMP BROCHETTES OR SURF AND TURF

½ lb. fresh or frozen shrimp, shelled

½ cup Heinz ketchup

¼ cup water

¼ cup onion, minced

1 tbsp. light brown sugar

3 tbsp. lemon juice

2 tbsp. vegetable oil

2 tsp. prepared mustard

2 tsp. Worcestershire sauce

½ tsp. chili powder

1 lb. beef sirloin steak cut into 1-inch pieces

8 small mushrooms, stemmed

2 small onions, quartered

1 green pepper, seeded and cubed

1 red pepper, seeded and cubed

6 cherry tomatoes

1 *Heat* grill to medium-hot.

2 If frozen, thaw shrimp. In a small saucepan *combine* the ketchup, water, onion, and brown sugar. Stir in the lemon juice, oil, mustard, Worcestershire sauce, and chili powder.

3 *Simmer* on a low heat uncovered 10 minutes, stirring occasionally.

4 On six skewers thread the sirloin pieces *alternating* with the shelled shrimp, mushrooms, onion wedges, and peppers. Grill kebobs

over medium-hot coals approximately 15–17 minutes for medium-rare or to desired doneness. Turn the kebobs often and brush with the sauce. Garnish the end of the skewers with tomatoes before serving.

SAVORY SCALLOP AND TURKEY BACON

½ **lemon, juiced**

½ **lemon rind, grated**

4 **tbsp. vegetable oil**

½ **tsp. dried dill**

12 **scallops**

6 **slices turkey bacon, cut in quarters lengthwise and crosswise**

1 **green bell pepper, seeded and cut into 1-inch pieces**

1 **red bell pepper, seeded and cut into 1-inch pieces**

1   Heat grill to hot. *Mix* together in medium nonreactive bowl lemon juice, rind, oil, and dill. Add the scallops and toss to coat. Marinate covered for 1½ hours in refrigerator. Remove the scallops from the marinade and discard marinade. Wrap a piece of bacon around each scallop.

2   *Thread* the bacon-wrapped scallops onto skewers alternating with the bell pepper pieces. Broil the skewers over hot coals for about 5–10 minutes, turning frequently until all sides are thoroughly cooked.

SERVES 4

SERVES 4

SIZZLIN' GARLIC SHRIMP

KEBOBS

12 ozs. raw shrimp, peeled

2 tbsp. fresh Italian flat leaf parsley or regular
   parsley, chopped

4 tbsp. lemon juice

salt and pepper to taste

2 tbsp. olive oil

5 tbsp. butter

3 small cloves garlic, minced

1 *Place* shrimp in shallow glass dish. In a small bowl combine parsley, lemon juice, and salt and pepper. Pour over shrimp and coat. Marinate in refrigerator for 45 minutes to 1 hour.

2 Heat the oil and butter in medium pan over medium heat and add garlic. *Mix* thoroughly until butter melts. Remove shrimp from marinade and add to pan and coat well, then thread shrimp onto several skewers.

3 Heat grill to hot. Broil kebobs over hot coals for 5–10 minutes, *turning* until the shrimp are pink and cooked through. Serve immediately.

J.R.'S TIP—*May be made in foil packets instead of skewers by placing shrimp onto a piece of aluminum foil, fold foil into thirds, and fold up ends completely, sealing. Open top to vent.*

HEART-HEALTHY TURKEY
CHILI

Pam cooking spray

1 medium onion, chopped

2 garlic cloves, minced

1 green pepper, seeded and chopped

1 lb. ground turkey

3 14-oz. cans stewed tomatoes, undrained and chopped

2 15-oz. cans Sylvia's pinto beans, rinsed and drained

⅓ cup mild salsa

⅓ cup mild picante sauce

1 tbsp. chili powder

1 tbsp. cumin

¼ tsp. red pepper flakes

1 tbsp. sugar

SERVES 4 - 6

1 *Spray* bottom of a large pot with Pam. Sauté onion, garlic, and pepper on medium heat. Add turkey and cook 10 minutes or until brown.

2 Add tomatoes, beans, salsa, picante sauce, chili powder, cumin, red pepper, sugar. Adjust seasonings to taste. *Simmer* for 30 minutes.

3 *Serve* with chopped onion, lite cheese and lite sour cream (optional).

RIO GRANDE BLACK BEAN CHILI

SERVES 6-8

2 cups dried black beans

water to cover

2½ tbsp. Crisco vegetable oil

3 onions, chopped

5 garlic cloves, minced

¼ cup chili powder

4 tsp. oregano

4 tsp. cumin

1 tsp. coriander

1 tbsp. paprika

¼ tsp. cayenne pepper

3 cups vegetable broth

1½ cups Delmonte canned diced tomatoes, undrained

½ can chipolte chiles, or to taste

3 cups water

1 tsp. white wine vinegar

5 tbsp. cilantro, finely chopped

salt and pepper to taste

1 *Rinse* and drain beans. Discard any stones. Place in a bowl and cover with water and let stand for 4–5 hours. Drain and set aside.

2 In a large pot, warm the oil over medium heat. Add onions and sauté until translucent. *Add* garlic, chili powder, oregano, cumin, coriander, paprika, cayenne pepper and stir to combine. Cook approximately 5 minutes. Add broth, tomatoes, chipolte, water, and beans

and bring to a boil. Reduce heat to low and cover partially and cook for 45 minutes.

3 Uncover and cook 35 minutes more. Add vinegar and cilantro. *Season* with salt and pepper to taste.

4 *Garnish* with lite cheese, lite sour cream, and cilantro.

J.R.'S TIP—When handling hot peppers, wear rubber or plastic gloves to protect hands, and avoid touching your face. Great with corn bread.

FLASH FRIED CATFISH

2 lbs. fresh catfish fillets

1 tsp. garlic powder

1½ tsp. salt

¼ tsp. ground pepper

2 cups cornmeal

½ cup olive oil

1 Rinse and pat dry the fillets. In medium bowl combine the garlic powder, salt, pepper, and cornmeal. *Dredge* the fillets in mixture so that it sticks to both sides of the fillets. Shake off the excess and set aside. On a medium-large heavy skillet heat oil on medium heat. Place fillets in pan and cook about 4–5 minutes until golden brown on both sides. Remove and drain on paper towels before serving.

J.R.'S TIP—The catfish fillets can be cut into strips for "catfish fingers."

SERVES 4

FAVORITE
OKLAHOMA
FOOTBALL MOMENTS

The closest I ever came to the Heisman Trophy was in 1987 in former O.U. coach Barry Switzer's office.

All the great, emotional battles with Texas and Nebraska come to mind. The numerous bowl games rank right up there, too. It's funny, but most OU fans truly do not like our neighbors down in Texas on the second Saturday in October, which is unique for me, because I have so many friends from Texas. But on that day, I join my brethren and pull for the Sooners with every fiber of my being to defeat the "enemy." **The Oklahoma-Cornhusker** rivalry is a little different, though. We want to win, of course, but there has never seemed to be the hatred. Though I don't like using that term, it's true, as it relates to the "other Big Red" to the north. Respect might be a better description for the OU–NU rivalry.

For some odd reason, my fellow broadcast colleague **Tazz**, who lives on Long Island in New York, is a huge Cornhusker fan. It seems strange for a city boy to be supportive of the big, red-faced, corn-fed boys from Lincoln, Nebraska. I wonder if the former resident of Red Hook likes BBQ?

Mom
my love
Jim
6-30-87

SERVES 4 CLASSIC COUNTRY FRIED STEAK

4 8-oz. rib eye steaks (fat trimmed)

6 tbsp. flour

½ tsp. salt

½ tsp. pepper (coarse ground)

1½ tsp. Lawry's season salt

½ tsp. paprika

½ tsp. garlic powder

2 eggs, lightly beaten

1 tbsp. olive oil

1 Combine flour, salt, pepper, season salt, paprika, and garlic powder in bowl.

2 Rinse and pat dry steaks. Dip in eggs and dredge in flour mixture, shaking off any excess flour. Heat 1 tbsp. oil in skillet over medium-low heat. Add steak, turning frequently until desired doneness.

J.R.'S TIP—*This is best cooked in an iron skillet, and served with Country White Gravy, page 91.*

FAVORITE SPORTS MOMENTS I HAVE SEEN

It is hard to beat the Oklahoma-Texas football game played every year in Dallas's Cotton Bowl on the second Saturday in October. It is during the annual Texas State Fair, the world's biggest, of course, on the Texas State Fairgrounds where the historic **Cotton Bowl** sits under the watchful eye of the venerable statue of Big Tex. Seventy-five thousand rabid football fans are equally dressed in Sooner crimson or Texas burnt orange, extremely vocal, some inebriated, usually on their feet for every play. The pure emotion and excitement of this game is hard to beat. The smell of corn dogs and other fare is dominant among the many sights and sounds of this Red River rivalry that affects virtually every person in both states.

I have been to over a dozen of these games in my life and have never been to another sporting event that quite compares. The 2000 Orange Bowl in Miami for the college football National Championship between Oklahoma and Florida State was another great sports moment I have experienced. I had the privilege of being on the OU sideline for that one, and my **Sooners** won the national championship that night, 13–2, over the always tough Seminoles. It was also my birthday, January 3, so it was the end of a perfect birthday, one I will never forget! The 2003 Rose Bowl where O.U. defeated Washington State was also a memorable day for me, especially because I had the priviledge of being on the Sooner sideline.

Professionally, **WrestleMania** is at the top of the list, as it is always the number one sports entertainment extravaganza of the year, with fans from all fifty states and many foreign countries always attending. These loyal fans' emotions have to be personally experienced to be believed. I always consider it a huge honor to be a part of this event.

Former Florida State University Seminole football great and WWE Superstar, Ron Simmons, and ol' J.R. on the sideline of the 2000 Orange Bowl.

MUSKOGEE MEAT LOAF

1½ lb. ground sirloin

½ cup Manero's steak sauce

½ cup Peter Luger steak sauce

1 tbsp. Worcestershire sauce

1 cup plain bread crumbs

2 eggs, beaten

sea salt and pepper (coarse ground) to taste

½ cup J.R.'s BBQ Sauce

1 tbsp. garlic powder

1 tsp. seasoned salt

1 tbsp. dried onions

¼ cup Heinz ketchup

1 *Preheat* oven to 350° F.

2 Mix all ingredients except the ketchup well. *Bake* in 8-to-9-inch loaf pan for 45 minutes at 350° F. Remove from oven and drain off fat. Top with the ketchup then bake for 15 minutes more.

3 *Serve* hot.

SERVES 6

J.D.'S VENISON STEW

SERVES 8

2 lbs. venison cubes or stew beef

2 tsp. seasoned salt

1 small clove garlic, chopped

½ tsp. pepper

1 tsp. crushed red pepper flakes or J.R.'s Hot Sauce

½ cup beer

water to cover

2 cups canned whole tomatoes, chopped, reserving liquid

2 large potatoes, unpeeled, cut into eighths

1 small cabbage, chopped

2 large onions, chopped

1 carrot, peeled and sliced

1 green pepper

1 *Mix* together salt, garlic, pepper, red pepper flakes. Place venison in a large pot and sprinkle half of the seasonings mixture over the meat. Pour in beer. Add just enough water to cover meat. On a medium heat, bring to boil. Reduce heat and simmer for 1½ to 2 hours or until tender. Add vegetables and remainder of the seasonings mixture and simmer on low 20 minutes.

JAN ROSS'S CHICKEN

CACCIATORE

SERVES 4

¾ cup all-purpose flour

2 tsp. dried oregano

1 tsp. dried basil

½ tsp. paprika

1 tsp. garlic powder

¼ tsp. salt

¼ tsp. pepper

1½ lbs. boneless and skinless chicken breasts

2 tbsp. olive oil

1 large onion, chopped

1 green pepper, seeded and chopped

1 red pepper, seeded and chopped

1 clove garlic, minced

2 14.5-oz. cans Del Monte stewed tomatoes with
   onion, basil, oregano

¾ tbsp. light brown sugar

1 In a small bowl, *combine* flour, oregano, basil, paprika, garlic powder, salt and pepper. Rinse chicken and cut into 1½-to-2-inch pieces. In a large nonstick skillet, heat olive oil.

2 Cook chicken turning pieces over until all sides are lightly browned, about 20 minutes. Remove chicken and set aside. Add to skillet onion, peppers, garlic and 1 tbsp. of oil. Saute 10–15 minutes until crisp tender. *Sprinkle* with flour/spice mix while cooking. Add tomatoes with juice and stir until bubbly. Add brown sugar. Continue to stir, add chicken to mixture. Cook 10–15 minutes more on low heat.

J.R.'S TIP—*Great with hot buttered noodles or rice.*

COMMITMENT MEANS WATERING THE DOG

My wife and business associates will tell you that I am just a little stubborn—ok, downright hardheaded! When I like something, I like it, and when I don't, I don't. It's that simple. There are few gray areas in my life. Goes back to what I was taught as a young man about learning the meaning of commitment and taking responsibility for one's actions. Your word has got to be your bond, and there was no room for lying at the **Ross Ponderosa** growing up. One bitterly cold Oklahoma winter day Dad had been working on his job for the Oklahoma State Highway Department for two or three days straight during a rare ice storm. With school closed due to the bad weather, I was home alone and left with the responsibility to take care of our farm animals, which included Dad's prize hunting dog. That means making sure the animals were fed and watered.

Problem was, I forgot to water the dog. Dad got to come home for a few minutes and asked me if I had done all my chores and I said yes, even though

My high school graduation photo from Westville, Oklahoma, in 1970. Now you know what a $3 haircut looks like!

I remembered I had not watered the dog. Dad went to check on things and found the dog's water bowl was frozen over. I had NOT watered the dog, but more importantly, I had lied to my father. Dad was 6 foot 3, 275 pounds in those days, and strong as a **Hereford bull**. He proceeded to take his belt off, take me outside in my stocking feet, and punish me for lying and not keeping my commitment. I got the message. I think Daddy cried that day, even more than his ten-year-old son, but I'll never know because he immediately took a long walk alone in the woods in front of our house and when he came back his eyes were very red. I think it broke his heart to have to teach me one of life's important lessons in the manner he did, but as I look back upon it, I am thankful for that day.

JAN'S SECRET SPAGHETTI  SAUCE

SERVES 6-8

¾ lb. sweet Italian sausage, cut into ½-inch pieces

½ lb. ground sirloin

½ lb. ground veal (optional)

¼ tsp. onion powder

¼ tsp. garlic powder

1 tbsp. olive oil

1 cup onion, chopped

¾ cup celery, chopped

2 cloves garlic, minced

1 tbsp. fresh parsley, chopped

1 tsp. basil, fresh or dried, chopped

1 tbsp. oregano, chopped, fresh or dried

1 tsp. onion powder

1 bay leaf

1 tsp. garlic powder

½ tsp. pepper

1 tbsp. Romano cheese

1 tbsp. Parmesan cheese

6–8 cans Contadina tomato sauce

1 tbsp. Contadina tomato paste

⅛ tsp. salt

1 tbsp. light brown sugar

1 In medium skillet, *brown* Italian sausage on medium-low heat until cooked through and browned. Drain. In a separate skillet cook on medium-low heat ground sirloin and veal and add onion powder and

garlic powder. Cook until browned. Drain. In a large pot, heat oil on medium-low heat. Add onion, celery, and garlic, and cook until onion is translucent, about 8 minutes, stirring occasionally. Add parsley and sauté 2 minutes. Add basil and oregano and stir constantly. Add onion powder, bay leaf, and garlic powder, stirring in pepper and cheeses. Cook 2 minutes, stirring constantly until just lightly browned. Add tomato sauce and paste and meats and stir until well combined, adding extra cheese if desired. Sprinkle brown sugar in and continue stirring. Cover and reduce heat to low and stir frequently. Simmer for 2–3 hours.

REAL COUNTRY COOKIN'

RABBIT

1 *Rinse* and cut rabbit into serving pieces.

2 Place rabbit in soup pot covered with water and **cook** until tender.

3 Remove from pot and flour pieces. Salt and *fry* in a skillet at medium heat.

My dad and his only son proudly displaying a sizable buck. I was only eight years old.

SQUIRREL

2 squirrels (remove the .22 bullets)

salt and pepper to taste

flour

6 tbsp. oil

2 cups water

1   *Cut* squirrel into several pieces. Place flour and seasoning in plastic bag. Place squirrel in bag and shake to coat.

2   Fry in skillet until golden. *Drain* and add water. Bring to a boil at low heat and simmer 1 hour.

FROG LEGS

1 egg beaten

½ cup cornmeal

½ tsp. sea salt

¼ tsp. pepper

2 lbs. frog legs

½ cup vegetable oil

1   Mix egg, cornmeal, salt and pepper into batter. *Dip* frog legs into batter and fry in oil in skillet on medium low for 25 minutes, turning occasionally to cook evenly.

Post-match "reflection" after a Hog-Pen match between Triple H and Henry Godwin. Notice the footwear.

THE MOST UNLIKELY-LOOKING STAR I EVER LAID EYES ON!

Yours truly, with the power-tie and suit, standard announcer attire in the eighties, interviewing the ultra-talented Mick Foley.

It took wrestling legend **Mick Foley** eleven long years of surviving hell in obscure places and paying his dues many times over to finally make it to the "big show." No, not that extra-large wrestler we have, I mean to WWE. That was largely because the powers that be in the company never felt that Mick *looked* like a star. The wrestler, turned double number one best-selling author, toiled for years on the independent circuit, in Japan and in Turner's WCW, before he finally got the opportunity to come to WWE in 1996.

I am happy to say that as vice president of talent relations, I was able to facilitate a meeting between Mick and **Vince McMahon** that lead to Vince hiring Mick and the two of them creating the character of Mankind. Mankind was a scary rascal with evil intentions who enjoyed making those around him miserable filling their lives with pain and agony. The exact and total opposite of Mrs. Foley's baby boy, and proud alum of Ward Melville High School on Long Island, New York.

When I first met Mick Foley, he was wrestling as **Cactus Jack**, a suicidal risk-taking daredevil who, at around 300 pounds, did things that 300-pound men would never dream of attempting to do, even on a dare. Cactus Jack was as fearless and hell-bent as any talent I have seen in over twenty-five years in this unique business.

I first met Cactus back in Dallas in 1987, at the "World Famous" Sportatorium ("at the corner of Cadiz and Industrial," as the former longtime voice of the Dallas Cowboys, **Bill Mercer**, would say). I had been told about this guy who did crazy but good things in the ring and that I needed to see him live. I was working for Turner's WCW but was still living in Dallas, so I went down to the matches one Friday night. After his match was over, I went in the back and met Cactus Jack, a Japanese kid named Super Black Ninja (later known worldwide as The Great Muta), and Percy Pringle, who WWE later hired and re-created as Paul Bearer.

I spoke about Cactus to **Jim Herd**, and Cactus was eventually brought into WCW. As a side note to historians, Mick's last match for World Class was in Ft. Worth, Texas, high on a scaffold, and Mick took the fall to the ring below, breaking his wrist in the process. Then, loading up his car in Texas and making the 900-mile drive to Atlanta, he was involved in a bad car wreck, which took his two front teeth out. So when he showed up for his Atlanta debut, he was pretty banged up. He wore a bridge for a while with new front teeth, but eventually that got left home and nobody missed 'em at all! It turned out that some of the **WCW** creative types weren't all that impressed with Mick's crazy style, as they said it killed credibility, because how could anybody take all that punishment and still get back up? Mick's gimmick was that he "loved pain." Mick once told me, "What idiot would love pain? That stuff hurts! I guess I just have a high-tolerance for it."

Behind the scenes, I always found Mick to be a class act, sensitive to the feelings of others, something some wrestlers are not familiar with whatsoever. Mick loved to perform for the fans, whether it was a high school of a couple of hundred fans or at **Madison Square Garden**, before a sellout crowd in the world's most famous arena. To be honest, I never thought Mick's career would last as long as it did, due to his insane style in the ring, complete with taking sickening chair shots to the head,

Former WWE Commissioner Mick Foley. Mick was a great success story in our company, but didn't spend too much money on his wardrobe.

being body-slammed on thumbtacks, and getting set on fire! This is all documented, folks.

Also, in my opinion, the manner in which Mick was portrayed in the documentary *Beyond the Mat* was not a totally accurate portrayal of Mick, or our business, but unfortunately some folks will always think that it is. Someday perhaps some enterprising TV executive will cast Mick as a modern-day **Ward Cleaver**, because nobody I know enjoys playing a dad in real life better than the former Dude Love.

He would be great at it on the small screen, I know. Mick continues to write novels in his garage with the same passion he displayed in the ring. He doesn't use a computer or typewriter but does it all in longhand and does it well. Mick and I have had our share of disagreements in my role as the head of talent, usually over financial issues, but at the end of the day, neither of us ever lost respect for each other, which is a rarity in the wrestling business. One of my proudest moments in this company was being able to hire **Mick Foley**, a kid I met at a small show in Texas, and look on in amazement as the guy with the "bad body" became a true worldwide star and double number one *New York Times* best-selling author.

J.R.'S "TAKE" ON THE NEW GENERATION OF WRESTLING ANNOUNCERS

We have the best young announcers in the sports entertainment biz with **Michael Cole**, Tazz (if that is your real name), and The Coach. Michael is a former newsman who covered major events around the world, including the Branch Davidian incident in Waco, Texas, a few years ago. Michael has been put in some tough spots over the years on our broadcasts, namely being positioned as a young upstart "heel" in a storyline that was ill-conceived and did not work. He has gotten past that blunder and is rapidly becoming a terrific broadcaster through his hard work and his study of the prod-

Tazz and Michael Cole are one of the best young announce teams we have ever had in WWE.

uct. I admire Michael for many reasons, namely his overwhelming work ethic and the fact he is a great family man.

Tazz is a former wrestler who gained prominence in the former ECW promotion based in South Philadelphia. A lifelong fan of the business, Tazz has been a classic overachiever his entire life and is becoming one of our business's best color commentators. Sometimes I think that Tazz's distinctive New York City accent is more pronounced than my Oklahoma drawl. Okay, maybe not. Michael and Tazz are the long-term future of our business when it comes to announcing and are establishing the measuring stick for all that will follow them. I hope that in some small way I have been able to help them, and I am certainly proud to be working with them in WWE.

The Coach is the consummate ladies man who never saw a game he would not bet on and is a bright, articulate young man who grew up in rural Kansas. There is no doubt in my mind that in time and with his continued hard work **Jonathan Coachman** will become an excellent play-by-play talent for the company. Coach came to us after being a sports anchor in Kansas City and learned a great deal working alongside NFL Hall of Famer, **Len Dawson**. Too bad his golf game sucks, or so says Bradshaw!

For the record, I must add that the King and I still love what we do and plan on doing it for many years to come, Good Lord willing.

Jonathan "The Coach" Coachman. Coach, a real ladies' man, lets me call him "Dawg."

Business is
about to
pick up!

WHO

WANTS

DESSERT?

SERVES 8 # CHEROKEE COUNTY CARROT CAKE

2 cups sugar

1 ½ cups vegetable oil

4 eggs

1 ¼ tsp. cinnamon or Cinnabon cinnamon

1 tsp. salt

2 tsp. baking soda

2 cups all-purpose flour

3 cups carrots, peeled and grated

½ cup walnuts, optional

1 15-oz. can Betty Crocker cream cheese frosting

1 *Preheat* oven to 350° F.

2 Grease and flour 13-x-9-x-2 pan. Mix sugar, oil, eggs, cinnamon, salt, and baking soda in large bowl. Add flour and mix. *Fold* in carrots and nuts. Bake for 40–45 minutes. Cool and frost with cream cheese frosting.

CANDY SHOPPE
SERVES 4 ## BBQ BAKED

APPLES

½ cup chopped walnuts

¼ cup sliced almonds

1 tbsp. light brown sugar

¼ cup chopped cherries

1 tbsp. Amaretto

4 medium apples (preferably Granny Smith)

2 tbsp. butter

1 *Heat* grill to medium.

2 In a small bowl *mix* together the walnuts, almonds, sugar, cherries, and Amaretto.

3 Core the apples. Place each apple on a large square of heavy or double thickness aluminum foil. *Spoon* the mixture into each apple, pushing gently into the hollowed-out core. Mound a little mixture on top of each apple. Dot apples with butter. Wrap apple in foil until completely closed. Cook the apples over medium-hot coals for 25–30 minutes or until tender.

J.R.'S TOP TEN FAVORITE MOMENTS FROM TED TURNER'S WCW

10 Working with some wonderful people. Not many, but some.

9 WCW head honcho Jim Herd pitching the "Hunchbacks" as an unbeatable tag team (two masked wrestlers with hunchbacks who could not be put flat on their shoulders, therefore they could not be pinned!).

From left to right: Jesse Ventura, Gordon Solie, Bruno Sammartino, Erik Watts, yours truly, and the Head of WCW, Cowboy Bill Watts, at the live *20th Anniversary of Wrestling on TBS* show in 1992.

8 Approving Jim Barnett's expense reports, where ties from Harrods "became" lunches.

7 Cowboy Bill Watts urinating off his twelfth-floor balcony and then bragging about it.

6 Jim Herd's tirades à la Artie on *The Larry Sanders Show*. They were EXACTLY the same, cussing and all!

5 The Ric Flair–Terry Funk series of matches, which were, for their times, barbaric bloodbaths.

4 The Ric Flair–Ricky Steamboat series of matches—that were almost too smooth.

3 Broadcasting *CLASH OF CHAMPIONS I*: Flair vs. Sting, in 1988 live on TBS. It was a history-making night for our business. Flair was awesome, and Sting was made.

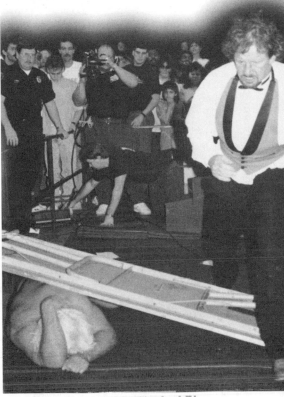

The ageless Terry Funk attacked Ric Flair using a table before they became fashionable.

2 Living in Atlanta, southern belles, and BBQ!

1 Getting the hell of there!

Steve Austin, before his "Stone Cold" days. Notice the Brian Pillman–inspired wrestling tights and the haircut.

J.R.'S TOP TEN
DEVIOUS DELIGHTS

10 Peanut butter pie (for Gorilla Monsoon)

9 Bread pudding **8** Carrot cake

7 Apple pie with cinnamon ice cream

6 Peach cobbler

5 Huckleberry cobbler

4 Linda McMahon's Hershey's pie

3 Homemade Ghiradelli chocolate chip cookies
(best thing my wife ever baked for me!)

2 Red velvet cake
(my birthday preference!)

1 Granny Mae's apple dumplings
with chocolate sauce

J.R.'S TOP TEN
"FEED ME MORE" LIST

10 Pinto beans with homemade corn bread and chopped purple onion, all in a large bowl together.

9 Homemade "cat's head" biscuits—eat 'em while they're hot, preferably with honey or apple butter!

8 New potatoes with fresh green beans—slow cooked together.

7 Pan-fried potatoes with purple or Vidalia onions.

6 Pot roast with plenty of 'taters, carrots, and onions.

5 Meat loaf with mashed potatoes.

4 BBQ chicken, with J.R.'s BBQ Sauce, of course.

3 Grilled trout, caught by my friend John Taylor, the finest attorney in Atlanta.

2 Grilled salmon (I challenge anyone to top my recipe for this one).

1 Steak—rib eye or flank, grilled to perfection.

BIG BAD BROILED COCONUT

PINEAPPLES

1 small pineapple

4 tbsp. unsalted butter

2 tbsp. light brown sugar

⅔ cup grated coconut

2 tbsp. rum

1 *Heat* grill to high.

2 Cut pineapple into quarters and remove core. Make horizontal cuts across the flesh of the quarters. *Melt* butter and brush over pineapple then sprinkle with sugar. Cover pineapple leaves to prevent burning and transfer to hot coals, cut side up. Broil about 10 minutes. Sprinkle with coconut and broil 5 minutes more. Remove from grill, spoon a little rum over pineapple, and serve.

SERVES 4

SMACKDOWN!

2 graham cracker squares or cinnamon graham crackers

½ plain chocolate bar (Hershey's)

1 large marshmallow

1. On a graham cracker, place 4 squares of the chocolate bar and 1 marshmallow. *Microwave* on high for 15 seconds or until slightly melted and top with second graham cracker. May be made on the grill too!

S'MORES

SERVES 1

SERVES 6

OKLAHOMA SOONERS STRAWBERRY PIE

1 9-inch Pillsbury pie shell

½ cup extra fine sugar

2 tbsp. cornstarch

¾ cup Tropicana orange juice

½ tsp. red food coloring

1 to 1½ pints strawberries, freshly washed, hulled, and halved

1 *Bake* pie shell following package directions.

2 In a small pot, *mix* sugar and cornstarch and then add orange juice and food coloring.

3 Cook over medium heat, stirring until clear. *Add* glaze to strawberries. Pour mixture into cooked pie shell.

4 *Refrigerate* until cold.

SWEET SUGAR CREAM

PIE

SERVES 8

½ cup sugar

½ cup light brown sugar

½ cup flour

pinch of salt

2 cups heavy cream

pinch of nutmeg

pinch of cinnamon

1 9-inch Pillsbury piecrust

1 *Preheat* oven to 400° F.

2 Mix in a medium bowl sugar, brown sugar, flour, and salt. Gradually add heavy cream. *Stir* in nutmeg, cinnamon. Pour into pie shell and bake for 15 minutes and then reduce heat to 350° F and bake for 20–25 minutes longer.

3 *Cool* completely. Pie filling will be loose but will thicken upon cooling.

OLD SOUTH PECAN PIE

SERVES 6

1 egg, slightly beaten

1 cup light Karo syrup

1 tsp. vanilla

½ cup sugar

pinch of sea salt

2 tbsp. butter, melted

2 tbsp. flour

½ cup milk

1 cup pecans, halved

1 9-inch Pillsbury piecrust

Preheat oven to 350° F. Mix eggs, syrup, vanilla, sugar, salt, and butter. Add flour and milk, then stir in pecans. Place piecrust in 9-inch pie pan. *Pour* mixture into piecrust. Bake at 350° F for 50–55 minutes.

CHOCOLATE CHIP

1 package butter supreme cake mix (Duncan Hines or
   Betty Crocker)

1 3-oz. package vanilla instant pudding mix

⅓ cup oil

¾ cup water

3 eggs

8 ozs. lite sour cream

1 6-oz. package chocolate chips

1 tbsp. flour

SERVES 8

1 **Preheat** oven to 350° F.

2 In a large bowl **blend** with a mixer cake mix, pudding mix, oil, water, eggs, and sour cream for 2 minutes.

3 In a plastic bag, put chocolate chips and flour and shake to coat. In a greased, floured bundt pan pour in half of the cake batter and then **add** chocolate chips, leaving excess flour in bag. Then add remainder of batter.

4 **Bake** until toothpick comes out clean, about 40–50 minutes.

FIZZY COLA CAKE

SERVES 8

2 cups sugar

2 cups flour

1½ cup miniature marshmallows

½ cup unsalted butter

½ cup Crisco oil

3¼ tbsp. Hersheys cocoa

1 cup Pepsi

½ cup buttermilk

1 tsp. baking soda

2 eggs, beaten

1 tsp. pure vanilla extract

1 Preheat oven to 350° F. Mix by hand sugar, flour, and marshmallows in medium bowl. **Combine** butter, Crisco, cocoa, and cola in saucepan and heat on low until melted. Pour over flour mixture and stir well.

2 Add remaining ingredients and *mix* well.

3 *Spoon* into greased 13-x-9-x-2-inch pan making sure all is distributed evenly. Bake at 350° F for 45 minutes. Remove to wire rack.

4 *Spread* on cola topping while hot.

FIZZY COLA TOPPING

½ cup butter

3¼ tbsp. Hershey's cocoa

6 tbsp. Pepsi

1 tsp. pure vanilla extract

1 box powdered sugar

1 cup chopped pecans or walnuts

About 10 minutes before the cake is done, combine butter, cocoa, and cola in medium saucepan and bring to a boil. Add in sugar. Remove from heat, stir in remaining ingredients. Mix until well combined. Pour over hot cake while still in pan. Will thicken as it cools.

SERVES 12 ALMOND JOY CAKE

1 10-oz. package Duncan Hines Milk Chocolate cake mix with pudding in the mix

1 15-oz. package Duncan Hines Home-Style Coconut Supreme Frosting

1 6-oz. package mini-chocolate chips, reserve 2 tbsp.

¾ cup chopped almonds, reserve 2 tbsp.

1 Make cake as directed on package.

2 Bake in 13-x-9-x-2-inch greased pan as directed.

3 Mix coconut frosting, chocolate chips, and almonds together and frost cooled cake. Top with almonds and additional chocolate chips.

4 **Variation:** For Mounds cake, substitute the milk chocolate cake mix with fudge cake mix and top with frosting, toasted coconut, and mini chocolate chips.

SERVES 8–10

CITY SLICKER AMARETTO-CHOCOLATE

CHEESECAKE

½ stick butter, melted

1½ cups Nilla wafers, crushed

3 oz. semisweet chocolate

2 8-oz. packages cream cheese, softened

3 eggs

1⅓ cups sugar

1 cup lite sour cream

½ to ¾ tsp. cinnamon or Cinnabon cinnamon

½ tsp. almond extract

2 tsp. Amaretto liqueur

toasted almonds, sliced

1 Preheat oven to 350° F. To make crust, mix Nilla wafer crumbs with melted butter. **Press** into the bottom of an 8- or 9-inch springform pan. Bake for 8 minutes and let cool.

2 *Melt* chocolate in medium bowl in microwave. Add softened cream cheese and heat until soft. In a food processor mix chocolate-cream cheese until smooth. Add eggs and sugar and mix together. Then add sour cream, cinnamon, almond extract, and Amaretto. Process until smooth.

3 Pour into crust and *bake* for 50–60 minutes.

4 Center should be slightly loose. **Remove** from oven, cool. Refrigerate for 3 hours.

J.R.'S TIP—*Check your owner's manual for the best temperature and time for melting the chocolate.*

PETER PAN RICE KRISPIES

1½ cups light Karo syrup

1½ cups sugar

4 tbsp. flour

2 cups Peter Pan peanut butter

1 tbsp. vanilla

1 box Rice Krispies (6 cups)

1 Mix together Karo syrup, sugar, and flour in a large pan. Over a medium heat, bring to a simmer. *Simmer* for 1 minute. Add peanut butter and vanilla. Stir together until it melts. Add box of Rice Krispies then pour and spread into 13-x-9-x-2-inch pan. Let cool and then cut into 12 squares.

TREATS

MAKES 12 TREATS

JAN'S FRESH BLUEBERRY TART

SERVES 6 - 8

TART PASTRY

2 cups flour

¼ tsp. salt

2 tbsp. sugar

12 tbsp. cold butter

2 egg yolks

2 tbsp. cold water

1 *Preheat* oven to 425° F.

2 Place flour, salt, and sugar in a medium bowl and mix. *Cut* butter into small pieces and mix into flour with a pastry blender until just combined. Add yolks and water. Blend until pastry pulls away from the sides of the bowl. Form dough into a ball and wrap in wax paper and refrigerate for 45 minutes.

3 Roll dough out on a lightly floured board. The pastry should be a little bigger than the pie pan or tart pan that you are using, since it will shrink a little when baked. Place in pan. *Line* the bottom of the shell with wax paper and add pie weights evenly to the pan. Place on baking sheet and bake for 10 minutes. Remove wax paper and weights. Return to oven and bake for 2 additional minutes. Cool.

BLUEBERRY CUSTARD FILLING

½ cup sugar

2 eggs

1½ lbs. blueberries, washed and drained

⅓ cup milk

⅓ cup heavy cream

½ tsp. vanilla extract

½ tsp. almond extract

1 *Preheat* oven to 375° F.

2 Combine sugar and eggs, beating well with a wire whisk. Add blueberries, milk, cream, vanilla and almond extracts, mix well. *Pour* into baked tart shell and bake for 40 minutes.

J.R.'S TIP—*Tart pastry can be made in a food processor.*

BABY RUTH

MAKES 24 COOKIES

½ cup butter

¾ cup sugar

1 egg

½ tsp. pure vanilla extract

2 1-oz. Baby Ruth bars cut into small pieces

1⅓ cup flour

½ tsp. baking soda

½ tsp. salt

1 Preheat oven to 375° F. *Cream* butter and sugar until smooth. Beat in egg. Then add remaining ingredients, stir.

2 *Drop* by ½ tsp. onto greased cookie sheet. Bake at 375° F for 10–12 minutes. Cool on wire rack.

TRAINING TABLE OATMEAL COOKIES

MAKES 12 COOKIES

1 cup all-purpose flour

½ cup flaked coconut

½ cup quick-cooking rolled oats or Quaker Oats Plain

1 tsp. baking soda

½ tsp. sea salt

¼ tsp. cinnamon or Cinnabon cinnamon

¾ cup light brown sugar, packed

6 tbsp. unsalted butter, soften

1 ripe banana, sliced

1 egg

¼ cup raisins

¼ cup dried apricots, chopped

⅓ cup chopped walnuts (optional)

1 *Preheat* oven to 325° F. Lightly grease baking sheet.

2 In a medium bowl, *stir* together flour, coconut, oats, soda, salt, and cinnamon.

3 In a large bowl *cream* brown sugar and butter until fluffy.

4 Add banana and egg and beat until *blended* with a fork. Stir in the flour mixture gently, about ½ cup at a time. And then fold in the raisins, and apricots, and the walnuts.

5 *Spoon* by tablespoonfuls onto the prepared baking sheet, spacing cookies 2 inches apart.

6 *Bake* 12–15 minutes or until golden. Cool on wire rack.

GEORGIA PEACH

SERVES 4

4 cups peeled and sliced peaches

⅔ cup plus 3 tbsp. Domino's superfine sugar

1 tsp. lemon rind, finely grated

½ tsp. almond extract

1 tbsp. lemon juice

1½ cups all-purpose flour

1 tbsp. baking powder

½ tsp. salt

⅓ cup vegetable shortening (Crisco)

1 egg

¼ cup milk

lite whipped cream (optional)

4 tbsp. peach schnapps (optional)

1 *Preheat* oven to 400° F. Butter a 2-quart baking dish.

2 Arrange peaches in dish. Sprinkle with ⅔ cup sugar, lemon rind, lemon juice, and almond extract. *Bake* for 20 minutes.

3 In the meantime, in a medium bowl, mix flour, 1 tbsp. sugar, baking powder, and salt. Mix in shortening until mixture is crumbly. Add milk and egg, mix until combined. *Remove* peaches from oven and drop dough by large spoonfuls over peaches. Sprinkle with remaining 2 tbsp. sugar. Return to oven for 15 minutes or until top is golden brown. Top with whip cream (optional) and/or drizzle with peach schnapps (optional) by dropfuls.

J.R.'S GRANNY'S APPLE DUMPLINGS WITH CHOCOLATE SYRUP

MAKES 6 DUMPLINGS

Sautéed Cinnamon Apples, page 96

pinch of nutmeg

1 10-oz. package Pepperidge Farm puff pastry shells

Hershey's chocolate syrup or Smuckers carmel syrup

1 *Preheat* oven to 400° F.

2 Place pastry shells on ungreased baking sheet and cook as directed for 20–25 minutes or until lightly browned. **Remove** top and fill each shell with Sautéed Cinnamon Apples and sprinkle with nutmeg. Replace top.

3 Remove to plate and *pour* chocolate syrup or carmel syrup, approximately 1 tbsp. on each pastry while hot.

4 *Serve* immediately.

"Authentically amazing undisputed champion"

MILE-HIGH NO-BAKE PEANUT BUTTER PIE

SERVES 6 - 8

1½ cup heavy cream

12 ozs. cream cheese, at room temperature

¾ cup extrafine sugar

1 cup peanut butter

1 tbsp. vanilla extract

1 9-in. Keebler chocolate piecrust

shaved chocolate

chopped peanuts

1 In a medium bowl *beat* heavy cream on medium speed until stiff. In a separate bowl beat cream cheese and sugar until smooth. Add peanut butter and vanilla to cream cheese mix and combine. Gently fold in whipped cream into cream cheese mixture until combined completely. Put in piecrust and top with shaved chocolate and peanuts. Refrigerate for 4 hours.

TOP **TEN** FAVORITE INTERNATIONAL CITIES TO VISIT

10 Sun City, South Africa

9 Amsterdam

8 Berlin

7 Dublin

6 Manchester, England

5 Calgary

4 Montreal

3 Tokyo

2 London

1 Toronto

This was before I lost my smile due to two bouts of Bell's palsy. I'm displaying my new camera in Tokyo, a gift from my then girlfriend, now wife, Jan.

From left to right: Arn Anderson, Ric Flair, Tony Schiavone, ol' J.R. without a hat, and Barry Windham in transit to a huge WCW event in 1991 at the Tokyo Dome. At this point we were all thinking, no more Japanese beer!

SERVES 6 J.R.'S CREAMY COCONUT CREAM

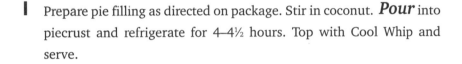

2 3-oz. pkgs. Jell-O vanilla cook & serve pie filling

3½ cups 2% milk

¼ to ½ cup coconut, shredded

1 9-inch Keebler shortbread piecrust

8 ozs. light Cool Whip

1 Prepare pie filling as directed on package. Stir in coconut. *Pour* into piecrust and refrigerate for 4–4½ hours. Top with Cool Whip and serve.

ADAIR COUNTY BLACKBERRY COBBLER

1 28-oz. jar blackberry pie filling, preferably Cracker Barrel

1 9-inch Pillsbury piecrust

1 tbsp. butter, melted

1 tbsp. sugar

1 *Preheat* oven to 400° F. In 8-x-8-inch square pan, pour in pie filling. Place piecrust on top, placing edges into pan. Pierce with fork 5 times.

2 Brush butter over crust. Then *sprinkle* sugar on top. Bake for 30 minutes until golden brown.

SERVES 4

SOUTHERN-STYLE
SERVES 4
BREAD
PUDDING

1 tbsp. butter

1 cup whole or 2% milk

6 slices of white bread, cut into cubes

1 cup extrafine sugar

¼ cup unsalted butter, softened

2 eggs

½ cup raisins

½ cup pineapple chunks, drained

½ cup coconut, shredded

½ tbsp. pure vanilla extract

⅛ tsp. cinnamon or Cinnabon cinnamon

¼ tsp. nutmeg

maple syrup (optional)

1 *Preheat* oven to 350° F.

2 Grease 8-inch square baking dish with 1 tbsp. butter. *Combine* in a medium bowl milk and bread and let stand. In a large bowl, cream sugar and butter. Beat in eggs. Mix raisins, pineapple, coconut, vanilla extract, cinnamon, nutmeg, and add to bread. Put into baking dish. Bake for 45 minutes until browned on top. Drizzle maple syrup on top if desired.

J.R.'S TIP—*May be made without the fruits.*

LIBATIONS AND DRINKS

GRANNY'S LEMONADE

⅔ cup sugar

1 cup boiling water

5 cups cold water

¾ cup freshly squeezed lemon juice (3 lemons)

1 lemon cut into slices

ice

mint (garnish)

Place the sugar in heat-proof 2-quart pitcher and add boiling water. *Dissolve* sugar by stirring. Add cold water, lemon juice and lemon slices. Serve over ice and add garnish.

MAKES 1½ QUARTS

SPARKLING HOMEMADE SODA POP

12-oz. can frozen concentrate juice (any flavor)

water

16-oz. bottle soda or seltzer

Mix together and add water to taste.

SERVES 2-3

SWANKY'S MALTED

2 scoops vanilla ice cream

1 scoop chocolate ice cream

1 tbsp. Carnation malt

1 tsp. Hershey's chocolate sauce

Blend in blender and serve immediatcly. Enjoy!

MILK SHAKE

SERVES 1

ICED COFFEE

3 cups fresh brewed Dunkin' Donuts coffee, cold

2 cups half-and-half, or milk of choice

2 tbsp. light brown sugar

2 cups crushed ice

Blend coffee, half-and-half, and sugar together. *Pour* over crushed ice.

SERVES 6

TOP **TEN** THINGS
THAT PAUL HEYMAN
DOES TO ANNOY PEOPLE

10 Never shines his cowboy boots.
(Why is he wearing boots anyway?)

9 Wears discounted suits from Moe Ginsburg.

8 Can dial a telephone
faster than any human alive.

7 Still lives with his parents,
even though he's thirty-something!

6 Wears his baseball cap backward, reminding
some of Seinfeld's friend, George Costanza.

5 Calls you on the phone when he KNOWS
you are NOT available, always leaving
a LONG message.

4 I heard this on his answering
machine once: "If this is you-know-who
calling about you-know-what, I'll call you
back as soon as I get this message."

3 **"I'll call you back in 5 minutes"**
—left on his answering machine for days on end.

2 **Dyes his hair so black, even more than**
the late Wahoo McDaniel did. Even darker than Elvis!

1 Continues to cultivate his lengthy ponytail
as if it had cultlike status. Hey, it could actually
mean something in Guyana!

Confrontation is great for television ratings. Here I am explaining to Heyman why he should cut the ponytail.

UNCLE HANK'S

SERVES 6 CUPS

KAHLUA

2 cups water

2 cups vodka

1 cup sugar

½ whole vanilla bean

1 oz. instant coffee crystals

Mix all the ingredients. Keep sealed in a dark place.

ICED COFFEE WITH

SERVES 4 - 6

A KICK

½ pot Dunkin' Donuts coffee

sweetener, your choice

KICK

1 strip lemon peel or

honey or

rum

KICK 2

Vanilla or coffee ice cream

Make coffee. Sweeten and cover, then refrigerate. When it reaches room temperature, add 1 strip of lemon peel, or honey or a small amount of rum. Coffee or vanilla ice cream is a great addition too!

OLD-FASHIONED
SOUTHERN

SUN TEA

4 cups cold water

2 large tea bags, black or herbal or combo

¼ cup sugar, Sweet'n Low, or Equal, or to taste

lemon or lime slices

ice cubes

1 Pour the cold water into a lidded 1-quart clear-glass container.

2 Place the tea bags in the water, leaving the strings dangling over the sides.

3 Cover and sit in direct sunlight for 3–4 hours. Add sugar, lemon, or lime slices. Pour over ice.

J.R.'S TIP—*You can add flavored syrups like blueberry, raspberry, or boysenberry to sweeten.*

SUMMERSLAM FRUIT PUNCH

½ quart unsweetened chilled pineapple juice

½ quart fresh chilled orange juice

½ quart chilled apple juice

1 quart chilled ginger ale

¼ gallon lime sherbert

1 **Pour** juices and ginger ale in punch bowl or large container.

2 **Top** with scoops of sherbet.

SERVES 25

BANANA SPLIT SHAKE

SERVES 4

½ cup milk

½ cup cream of coconut

1 small banana, sliced

10 maraschino cherries

1 tbsp. unsweetened cocoa

3 cups vanilla ice cream

1 In blender **combine** milk, cream of coconut, banana, 6 cherries, and cocoa.

2 **Cover** and process at high speed until smooth.

3 Add ice cream and **blend** at medium speed until smooth.

4 **Garnish** with a cherry and serve immediately.

YUMMY BANANA SMOOTHIEEEHA!

1 cup whole milk, or 2%

½ cup mashed banana

½ cup banana liqueur

⅓ cup Hershey's chocolate-flavored syrup

2 cups crushed ice

1 Place all ingredients in blender except ice. Cover and *blend* on high speed 2 minutes.

2 *Decrease* speed and blend 1 minute.

3 *Serve* immediately over crushed ice.

SERVES 3

TEXAS RATTLESNAKE HOT TODDY

3 cans or bottles of Dr Pepper

3 thin lemon slices (whole round slices)

1 In medium saucepan on medium heat, pour in Dr Pepper until heated through. Pour into mugs and top with whole lemon slices. Serve hot.

SERVES 3

A Cotton Bowl Tradition—In the cold of winter, this hot sweet drink was served to fans sitting in the cold at Dallas Cowboy games at the Dallas Cotton Bowl in the 1960s and 1970s. Maybe it still is. It was sold by roaming vendors who would squirt you a steaming cupful out of a big futuristic hot bottle gimmick they had on their back. The cups already had the slice of lemon on the bottom of each cup and it floated to the top. I think it was a buck and they sold all they could haul.

ROOT BEER

FLOAT

1 1-liter bottle of IBC, Dr. Brown's or A&W root beer

2 scoops of Ben & Jerry's vanilla ice cream

maraschino cherries for garnish (optional)

1 Place 1 scoop of ice cream in a tall glass and then top with root beer until it reaches the top of the glass. *Garnish* with cherry, if desired

SERVES 2

FROSTY RASPBERRY
CHAMPAGNE

PUNCH

SERVES 8

1 10-oz. package frozen red raspberries, thawed

2 tbsp. lemon juice concentrate

¼ cup sugar

½ bottle chilled red rose wine

½ quart raspberry sherbet

½ bottle champagne

1 In a blender, *combine* raspberries, lemon juice, sugar.

2 In a large pitcher, add wine to raspberry mix and *stir* gently while adding sherbet and champagne. Serve immediately.

THE TALL MAN FROM TEXAS SAID, "J.R., I WANT TO GET A BOOB JOB!"

No two days seem to be ever the same in the sports entertainment business, which always keeps things interesting. Indeed, never a dull moment in WWE! As a matter of fact, some days are downright bizarre.

I was sitting in a small makeshift office/dressing room in **Madison Square Garden** a few hours prior to a televised event a few years ago preparing for that night's show, when I heard a knock on my door and yelled, "It's open."

In walks the 6-foot-5, 260-pound Goldust, who was born Dustin Runnels, the son of the famous "American Dream" **Dusty Rhodes**, who by the way was one of the most charismatic wrestlers of all time. Dustin had been portraying the gold-clad, controversial character Goldust for quite some time, and the creative energy for the character was beginning to seemingly run its course. The creative staff were finding themselves scratching their heads, attempting to find fresh ideas for the Texas-born athlete. Goldust was usually accompanied to ringside with his then-real-life wife, Terri (they have since divorced), who portrayed the character Marlena, a sexy, cigar-smoking accomplice who balanced her counterpart's alleged "alternative lifestyle."

Goldust had a very good "run," as is said in the business, including a significant payday for working with **"Rowdy" Roddy Piper** in the "Hollywood Backlot Brawl" at *WrestleMania XII* in Anaheim, California, on March 31, 1996. Complete with an O. J. Simpson–inspired white Ford Bronco as a chase vehicle, this match had a little bit of everything, including a great effort by both performers.

In any event, the hot creative ideas were slowing for the Goldust character, and we had all been brainstorming for new ideas. Dustin comes in to the small room at MSG, takes a seat, and proceeds to tell me that he has *the idea* that will put him back on the map. With a film crew present, he wants to go under the knife and have a breast implant procedure, essentially making him the first she-male character in sports entertainment history! His vision was that it would be so weird and bizarre that our fans and new fans, for that matter, would pay good money to watch him wrestle. He suggested that he would be huge on the talk show circuit, and people all over the world would be clamoring to see the **"Bizarre One"** in person (especially in prison, and perhaps in Amsterdam!).

I was shocked at what I was hearing. Here I am, this Oklahoma farm boy sitting in New York City's Madison Square Garden having one of the most unique conversations of my life with a large man with a bleached blond buzz cut, who wants to get a bona fide boob job!

I said, "**Dustin**, what about when you're not at work? I mean, these new boobs don't snap on and off. They are permanent until you have *another* surgery to have them removed. What do you do with them when you take your daughter to school? What happens to your two new additions when you attend a PTA meeting? You would pretty much eliminate taking the family on outings to the beach if you do this, wouldn't you think?"

He indicated it would be worth the sacrifice, because this character would be the hottest new thing in the world and the money would be rolling in for everyone! I said that we really needed to speak to

Vince McMahon, the chairman of WWE, on this one, as I did not feel comfortable approving this elective surgery from my talent relations budget. Contrary to what you might think, even though other members of our talent roster have had breast enhancement surgeries, they have all been women and have paid for their own "additional freight."

I took Dustin to Vince's customary office, which he always has at MSG events, and said, "Vince, Dustin has an idea he wants to pitch you about his Goldust character." "Great," said the boss as he sat down to listen to what I'm sure he was hoping would be the idea to get the "Bizarre One's" career on track again. Dustin began to describe the concept with all the convictions of an overcaffeined Jimmy Swaggart on a Sunday morning. Vince had an astonished look on his face and as he told me later, he thought he was being "ribbed." It was no rib, and after Dustin finished, Vince explained that he appreciated Dustin attempting to come up with new concepts for the character and to continue to brainstorm on them, but that Vince did not think this particular creative idea was the direction we wanted to travel. Later I asked **Goldust's** then-wife, Terri, if she knew about his concept, and she answered by rolling her eyes and nodding her head. That pretty well covered it.

Every time, to this very day, that I hear the *Crying Game* theme, I think of that bizarre day in Madison Square Garden where a 6-foot-5, 260-pound man asked me to authorize a boob job! Thank goodness we didn't do it, and Goldust's career has continued very well without the "enhancement."

SERVES 10-12

SUNDOWN SANGRIA

1 orange, sliced and seeded

1 lemon, sliced and seeded

1 peach, peeled and sliced

⅓ cup fresh strawberries

2 tsp. sugar

2 oz. peach brandy or fruit-flavored brandy

1 1-liter bottle red wine

ice

1 Add the 4 fruits to a large pitcher. Mix sugar and brandy and pour over fruit. Let stand for 4 hours.

2 At serving time, add 1 bottle of red wine and ice. Stir until cold.

3 May serve in chilled goblets if desired.

SPICY BLOODY MOLLY

1⅓ cup vodka

1⅓ cup Campbell's tomato juice

1⅓ cup V-8 juice

½ oz. Worcestershire sauce

10 drops Tabasco sauce, or J.R.'s Hot Sauce to taste

½ tsp. salt

juice of ½ lime

black pepper to taste

ice

SERVES 6

1 Mix all ingredients in large container. Serve over ice.

J.R.'S TOP TEN FAVORITE TAG TEAMS OF ALL TIME

10. The Kentuckians. Grizzly Smith and Luke Brown were two huge, bearded mountain men–type performers who, at the time in the 1960s, were the two biggest wrestlers I had ever seen. Grizzly, the father of Jake "The Snake" Roberts, was 6 foot 10, while his partner was around 6 foot 7, with both weighing in at well over 300 pounds each. They had one of the most famous tag-team rivalries with the Assassins ever in the business. It is a feud that occurred when I was around ten or twelve years old and I can still vividly remember it!

9. Bret and Owen Hart. I did not have the privilege to see them over a long period of time, as they were usually with other partners or in singles matches, but without a doubt, these two sons of the legendary Stu Hart of Calgary, Alberta, Canada, were simply amazing! There is no doubt in my mind, if fate had dealt these two athletes a different hand they could

Owen Hart & Bret Hart.

have been the greatest team ever. Someday I would love to go on a long ride with Bret and discuss our lives and individual journeys in our business.

8. The Blackjacks with Bobby "The Brain" Heenan. Black Jack Lanza and Black Jack Mulligan (Bob Windham) were black cowboy hat–wearing, cowboy-boot-stomping, rugged hombres who drew money wherever they went, and were as believable as any team I think I ever saw. They had great ring psychology and physicality, and when you added their all-world manager, Bobby "The Brain" Heenan, to the equation, you had pure magic. Jack Lanza, to this very day, still has a great wrestling mind and is another of my mentors.

7. Dick Murdoch and Dusty Rhodes. The world renowned "Texas Outlaws" were so far ahead of their time, it wasn't even funny. They were two of the most talented and charismatic wrestlers I ever saw, who could work any style and could out-talk any tag team of their generation. They "lived their gimmick," as the cliché goes, as they loved to drink beer, listen to country music, and raise hell. In Canyon, Texas, they were more famous than fellow West Texas State alumni, former Miami Dolphin, Mercury Morris.

Dick Murdoch.

6. The Four Horsemen. This dominant team had several incarnations that always included Ric Flair, Arn Anderson, and Tully Blanchard along with other partners, like Ole Anderson and Lex Luger. Arn Anderson, one of the very best tag-team wrestlers I ever saw, and Blanchard, another West Texas alumni, might have been the best duo of the group in their prime, because Flair was largely a singles wrestler. Ole Anderson was also an amazing tag wrestler, but I did not have the privilege of seeing him as much in person as I did Arn

Arn Anderson & Ric Flair.

and Tully. Incarnations of the Horsemen toward the end of their run had Sid Vicious and even Sting as part of their crew. The final version of the Four Horsemen featured the Canadian Crippler, Chris Benoit.

5. The Fabulous Freebirds. Michael "P.S." Hayes, Terry "Bam Bam" Gordy, and Buddy Roberts were lightning in a bottle, who portrayed hell-

Buddy Roberts , Michael "P.S." Hayes & Terry "Bam Bam" Gordy.

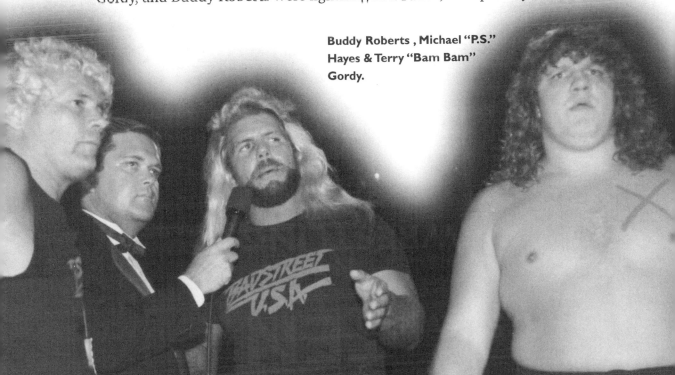

raising, ass-kicking, partiers who cared about no one but themselves, and man, did they live their "gimmick" to the hilt away from the ring! Their story line with the Junkyard Dog in the 1980s was one of the most intense reality-based issues I have ever personally witnessed. Hayes was a heat-seeking missile on the microphone. Gordy was an amazing talent who started in the business at age fifteen and he was very good even then. And Roberts was a veteran who complemented the younger team members' style perfectly. This trio's battles with the Von Erich brothers in Texas is also the stuff of legend. Sometimes the 'Birds were a pain in the backside to deal with, but they sold tickets!

4. Rock 'n' Roll Express.

Ricky Morton and Robert Gibson were the consummate baby face tag team when they lit territories on fire in the 1980s. Ricky was so convincing when he was being punished by an adversary in the ring, that I have literally seen women at ringside break down and cry, and even faint, they were so concerned for his safety and welfare. Robert was a great complement to the charismatic Morton. Both were great students of the game, and I only wish more teams in today's marketplace would study their tapes and their feud with the Midnight Express to see how a tag team match should be presented.

Ricky Morton & Robert Gibson.

3. Midnight Express with Jim Cornette.

They were controversially innovative and ahead of their time in the 1980s, with their tennis racket–

Stan Lane & Bobby Eaton flank James E. Cornette.

carrying manager, Jim Cornette, leading the way with the best antagonist promos on television of the era. Bobby Eaton and Dennis Condrey were poetry in motion and conducted a clinic most every night they went to the ring. These two loved to generate raw, animalistic emotion from the audience, and did it on a regular basis. For a villain team to be successful, the fans must want to pay their hard-earned money to see them get their butts kicked, and the 'Express did just that on a regular basis. When Condrey left and Cornette replaced him with Sweet Stan Lane, the team never really missed a beat. Great chemistry and great heat! Eaton may be the most underrated tag wrestler in history.

2. The Assassins. They were a masked, villain team I first saw in the famous rivalry with the Kentuckians, when I was only ten or twelve years old in Oklahoma. Jody Hamilton, the father of WWE referee Nick Patrick, and his partner, Tom Renesto, were the most significant "heel" team I think I ever saw, because almost forty years later I can still remember their menacing promos and their flawless, yet deadly, tag-team style. Their presence on TV caused me many a bad dream as a youngster.

1. Jack and Gerry Brisco. My two favorite brothers from my home state of Oklahoma were as smooth as any team ever, and were equally as good as fan favorites or heels. Both were great mat wrestlers and had uncanny ring psychology, no matter their role in the match. Any young wrestlers wanting to make their mark in our business would be well served to watch as many tapes of the Briscos in tag action as possible. Both of these Native Americans were also outstanding individual wrestlers, especially Jack, who was a tremendous NWA World's Heavyweight Champion in the old NWA heyday.

Yours truly, with wrestling legend Gerald Brisco.

TEN COMMON MISCONCEPTIONS ABOUT WRESTLERS

10 The wrestlers are all best friends.

9 The wrestlers always travel together in the same car.

8 They always use "blood capsules."

7 Wrestlers NEVER get hurt.

6 Wrestlers rehearse for hours before performing.

5 Wrestlers are like circus animals and always do as they are instructed.

4 Wrestlers are all dumb jocks.

3 Wrestlers could not make it in the "real world."

2 Wrestlers stay in character at home with the wife and kids.

1 Wrestlers do not own laptops.

TOP **TEN** FUNNIEST TALENT I'VE SEEN IN MY CAREER

10 Pat Patterson and Gerald Brisco—Both with their distinctive accents, they were classic corporate butt-kissers for Mr. "Mac-Man," but **PLEASE**, no more "in-drag" scenarios for the "Stooges."

Pat Patterson and Gerald Brisco (in the Brisco Brothers Body Shop t-shirt).

9 Dean Malenko—WWE's answer to Henny Youngman. Jackie Mason has nothing on this second-generation star. One funny Lansman!

8 General Skandor Akbar—The squatty fullback of the Vernon, Texas Lions portrayed a sinister Lebanese strongman most of his career—even with his Texas drawl!

General Sandor Akbar was my first traveling partner.

7 Bradshaw—Has picked up where the late Dick Murdoch, another Texan, left off, except Bradshaw, with his college education, is more, uh, refined.

6 Steve Austin, Rock, and Triple H— All are quick-witted with great, natural comedic timing, and each can do it all with a straight face.

Interviewing the one and only "Texas Rattlesnake," Stone Cold Steve Austin.

Bobby "The Brain" Heenan and the late great Gorilla Monsoon.

5 Gorilla Monsoon—**A hilarious straight man for** "The Brain," **among others. Often had a Don Rickles–like delivery. Car trips with Gorilla and Heenan were priceless.**

4 Jim Cornette—

Jim is like **Eb, of** Green Acres **fame, on a double latte! Another great one-liner guy, who's never at a loss for words. "R-rated" stand-up, tailor-made for the** Grand Ole Opry, **but he would shock the blue-haired old ladies out of their walkers.**

This outfit is not fire retardant! Jim Cornette.

3 The King—**I have heard some of his one-liners a dozen times and I still laugh. He's naturally funny with great recall and timing. King loves life and has become like a brother to me . . . an older brother.**

Jim Carey, who portrayed Andy Kaufman in Man on the Moon, was as goofy as a pet coon off the movie set as on it. That's me trying to figure out what's about to happen, along with Stacy Carter, the King's ex, and Jerry Lawler.

2 Bobby Heenan—**A comic genius! No one loves to make people laugh more than** "The Brain." **He's Mr. Ad-Lib!**

1 Owen Hart—The King of the Ribbers! **Seemingly spent every waking moment planning another joke to pull on some unsuspecting soul.**

Owen Hart (right) was poetry in motion in the wrestling ring.

TOP TEN THINGS THAT WOULD SURPRISE YOU ABOUT WWE SUPERSTARS

10 Most have been fans of wrestling all their lives.

9 They are home owners. (No, they don't live out of their cars.)

8 Most make regular trips to the dentist.

7 Most have children they are aware of.

6 Most train at least four days a week in a gym.

5 Many have financial planners.

4 Most own more sweatpants than anyone on their block, including hundreds of free T-shirts.

3 They have more frequent flyer miles than anyone you know.

2 Know where all the best buffets are in America.

1 Have attended college (no, not just trade schools), and many have graduated.

JYD—A CHAMPION OF HIS PEOPLE AND A VICTIM OF HIS SUCCESS

For my money, the **Junkyard Dog, aka Sylvester Ritter,** was the greatest black star in the history of the wrestling business. Also he befriended a young wrestling announcer from Oklahoma in the early 1980s in the old Mid South Wrestling territory, owned and op erated by one of my mentors, **Cowboy Bill Watts.**

Watts, who some critics considered a racist (mistakenly so, in my view), took a great deal of heat from his fellow Caucasian promoters around the country for anointing a black man as his top star. Cowboy was a brilliant man in many ways, and marketing

The late Sylvester Ritter was a hugely successful hero in Mid South Wrestling. When JYD came to the WWE, his charisma made him world famous.

was one of them. He realized that in the Mid South territory that consisted of cities in Louisiana and Mississippi, plus Oklahoma and Arkansas, that our fan base was made up of many African-Americans. With the invaluable help of his booker at the time, **Ernie "the Big Cat" Ladd,** another African-American, Cowboy knew he could strike gold if he could create a wrestling character that the black audience could identify with and believe in.

Consequently, JYD was created and put in a position that no other black man had ever been given the opportunity to have, the lead baby face—or hero—in a major wrestling territory. With his signature **"Another One Bites the Dust"** entrance music, the 6-foot-3, 280-pound former college football lineman from Fayetteville State University had awesome charisma, but limited pure wrestling skills. He worked hard and became a box office sensation and carried the territory on his broad shoulders for several years. The formula was simple, looking back on it. With JYD as the resident hero, a heel—or villain—factory was put in place to manufacture a constant flow of adversaries for the Dog.

It worked to perfection. Box office records were broken in virtually every city in the territory, and thanks largely to the crowds JYD was drawing, the wrestlers all made a decent buck. TV ratings in the area were staggering, with some stations delivering up to a 50 share in their time slots, often exceeding the station's local newscasts!

JYD, with a college degree in history and political science, was not a dumb jock, and with his intelligence and natural wit he became one of the classic interview talents I have ever been around. He was also a bighearted rascal who often helped needy families with his financial generosity and moral support. At one point, he was the most popular pro athlete in the state of Louisiana, at the same time Archie Manning was playing quarterback for the Saints and Pistol Pete Maravich was averaging 30 points a night for the then-New Orleans Jazz of the NBA. Anyone who had the privilege of knowing the Dog loved him. He genuinely cared for people but was virtually destitute as a result of his ongoing battle with drugs when he died in a tragic car accident on June 2, 1998, while on his way home from attending his daughter's high school graduation. He was killed when he fell asleep behind the wheel and crashed his 1996 Nissan while driving on I-20 from Louisiana to his home in Charlotte, North Carolina. Sylvester Ritter, known in the wrestling world as **Junkyard Dog,** was forty-five.

JYD was so famous in that part of North Carolina that even NBA legend and North Carolina native Michael Jordan sent his condolences to the funeral services. One of my biggest regrets in my professional life was that I did not attend the funeral service of the Junkyard Dog due to a scheduling conflict. I should have been there to pay my respects. Many of us inside the business should have tried harder to help him overcome his demons, but more often than not, he did not want the help. He was a proud man, and as I spoke to him one of the last times I saw him, in Atlanta in the early 1990s, he spoke of his problems and said that he got himself in the "mess I am in" and that he would get himself out. We oftentimes kidded him about being the **"Junk FOOD" Dog,** as he loved candy bars and virtually anything else that was sold in vending machines found in hotels. He had his good friend and confidant, referee Randy "Pee Wee" Anderson, who passed away a year or so ago, traveled with him more often than not, and **"Pee Wee"** always carried a huge bag of coins with him to make sure that if JYD got the munchies in the middle of the night, that Anderson would always have an adequate amount of change to feed the vending machines.

I like to think that JYD is in heaven now, with his ever-present smile and feeling proud that he was not only a great friend to all who knew him, but also that he blazed the trail that other African-American athletes in our business have been able to travel ever since. I can still vividly remember the downtown Municipal Auditorium in New Orleans rocking on a Monday night with the chant, *"Who gonna beat dat Dog? Who dat?!"*

Fame, however, did not come without a price.

the greatest black star in the history of the wrestling business

WE'RE ALL PLAYING FOR SECOND PLACE

He broadcast over 25,000 matches, and from 1973–85 was the unmistakable voice of Georgia Championship Wrestling, followed by **World Championship Wrestling,** on SuperStation TBS. He started his career earning five dollars a night doing ring announcing in Tampa, and ended it as the greatest wrestling commentator of all time. Gordon Solie, for my money, was the best to ever grace a broadcast booth in our profession. He was the **"Dean."** He was my advisor. He was my broadcasting role model in this business.

After serving our business so proudly for most of his adult life, and then being basically forced to the sidelines by pathetic wrestling politics,

Gordon Solie and yours truly, broadcasting *Clash of the Champions IX,* **a live prime-time television special, on November 15, 1989.**

I had the privilege of getting Turner's WCW to hire Gordon back to TBS in 1989, where he remained until 1995.

It is one of my proudest moments in this business to be able to repay this man in a small way for the influence he had on my career. The sad, oftentimes dark underbelly of this business put the **Dean** on the bench much too early, in my view. The way he was treated in Turner's WCW the last couple of years he was there, and after I had left to come to WWE, was an embarrassment that I am relatively sure Ted himself was unaware of.

I studied Gordon's call of the July 11, 1964, Danny Hodge–Hiro Matsuda junior-heavyweight title match from Tampa literally dozens of times while serving my apprenticeship for Oklahoma promoter **Leroy McGuirk** in Tulsa in 1973. McGuirk was blind and Gordon's call of the match allowed Leroy to "see" what was going on in this all-time mat classic. The first time I heard Gordon call this famous match I was twelve years old, and I never forgot it.

From that day until today, I have strived to be able to add realism and authenticity to every match that lends itself to that style, thanks to the precedent set by **Gordon Solie.** As a matter of fact, my first broadcast partner was Mr. McGuirk, and with him having no sight, I had to be very descriptive and thorough with my calls so he could relate to what was transpiring in the ring. One of the nicest things, I believe, Leroy ever said to me was that if I continued to improve, worked hard, and always respected the business, someday I might be as good as Gordon Solie.

Gordon passed away on July 28, 2000, from cancer at the age of seventy-one, but we had a wonderfully rewarding night together reminiscing at the fiftieth anniversary of the **NWA** function in Cherry Hill, New Jersey, a few months before he died. I was there to say some words about my mentor and friend, Gordon Solie, and I said a lot of them and meant every word. Gordon was ill, so he sat in the audience with all the great NWA legends and soaked up the love that people were sending his way. Afterward we sat at the bar and had one, or three, for the road. When we left each other for the last time, I told him, "Thank you from the bottom of my heart for all you have done for me and our business." We laughed and even cried about our experiences together in WCW, and I made sure he knew that he would always be the best broadcaster ever—and that the rest of us are simply playing for second place.

the greatest
wrestling commentator
of all time

J.R.'S TOP TEN FAVORITE ANNOUNCER/COMMENTATORS IN WRESTLING HISTORY

10 Paul "E." Heyman—so easy to dislike as a heel broadcaster. Intelligent and high-strung. Challenging, yet fun to work with.

9 "Mean" Gene Okerlund—perfected the art of the straight man/wrestler stand-up interview. Gene had more charisma and timing than most he interviewed. (Love his "Mean Gene Burgers.")

8 Michael Hayes—a great villain as one of the hated Freebirds, who knew his role and did it very well. I thought we had a great chemistry in the 1980s.

Sometimes even Paul and I are both speechless as some of the antics are played out in front of out eyes.

7 Bob Caudle—wonderful North Carolina gentleman from my NWA days who was underrated and a great partner. Bob was friendly to me while others in the old NWA gave me the cold shoulder, when I first arrived there.

6 Lance Russell—a class act. A southern legend who could have been a national hit if he had left Memphis sooner, and he had great chemistry with the King.

Two class acts, veteran wrestling announcers Lance Russell and Bob Caudle.

5 Bob Marella, a powerful amateur heavyweight wrestler at Ithaca College, became Gorilla Monsoon, a legendary wrestling personality.

Gorilla Monsoon—a wonderful man with a huge heart who treated me like a son. I sincerely wish his twin grandsons could have gotten to know him.

4 Jim Cornette—brilliant mind, passionate, and real old school, then and now. He knows how to get talent "over." Was like an "evil" Jerry Clower.

3 Bobby "The Brain" Heenan—as talented and funny as any partner I ever had. We both loved the chocolate cake and an occasional beverage together.

2 Jerry "the King" Lawler—my friend and one of the funniest men I've ever known. Stress-free and will probably live to be a hundred. He's the world's oldest teenager. (Sorry, Dick Clark!)

"Wease" to his friends, and "Weasel" to the fans: Bobby "The Brain" Heenan.

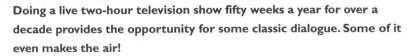

Doing a live two-hour television show fifty weeks a year for over a decade provides the opportunity for some classic dialogue. Some of it even makes the air!

1 Gordon Solie—the absolute BEST. The rest of us are all fighting for number two. I would drive for miles as a young man just to hear "The Dean" on cable station WTBS on Saturdays at 6:05 P.M. EST. He taught me so much, and I cherish the time we spent together.

J.R.'S TOP **TEN** EMOTIONAL MOMENTS AT RINGSIDE

10 My return **from Bell's palsy at** *WrestleMania XV*, **March 28, 1999, in Philadelphia:** Rock vs. Austin. What a match and what a night!

9 Bobby Heenan **leaving** *Raw* **for the last time.**

8 Owen Hart pile-driving Stone Cold **and almost crippling the Texas Rattlesnake.**

My return to work after my second bout with Bell's palsy. I received over 10,000 cards and letters while I was sidelined.

7 The Rock's family celebrating with tears in their eyes at ringside, after Rock won the WWF title for the first time.

6 Mick Foley, after losing to Triple H in a Loser-Leaves-Town match, waving good-bye to the fans just before he walked through the curtains, we thought for the last time.

5 Mick Foley at *King of the Ring* in Pittsburgh, and leaping off the Hell in the Cell cage to give our fans a moment that none of us will ever forget.

4 Hollywood Hulk Hogan in Montreal, March 18, 2002; the day after *WrestleMania X8*. Even the veteran Hulkster shed a tear.

3 Ric Flair—in his hometown of Charlotte, North Carolina, on his return to WWE, with a much-deserved standing "O" for perhaps the best ever.

The awesome, unforgiving steel structure has been the site of some hellacious battles, but none will ever overshadow the Undertaker and Mick "Mankind" Foley match.

2 Droz's accident in a match in Nassau Coliseum that left him confined to a wheelchair, for now.

1 Owen Hart's accident in Kansas City, May 23, 1999, a day I will never forget.

"I don't mind telling you that I cried real tears during many of these situations."—J.R.

TOP TEN FAVORITE RESTAURANTS TO EAT AT ON THE ROAD

10 13 Coins—Seattle, Washington

9 Papacito's—Houston, Texas

8 Smith and Wolensky's—New York City and Las Vegas

7 Arthur Bryant's BBQ—Kansas City, Missourri

6 Sylvia's—New York City

5 Fat Matt's Rib Shack—Atlanta, Georgia

4 Swanky Frank's—Norwalk, Connecticut

3 Rib Crib—Oklahoma City and Tulsa, Oklahoma

2 Earl's BBQ—Oklahoma City, Oklahoma

1 Morton's

ENGELBERT HUMPERDINCK, DAMMIT, THE NEW NWA CHAMPION!!

It was in the early 1970s, and I had just gotten into the business and was sitting in a small office in the Tulsa, Oklahoma, Convention Center that housed Championship Wrestling, owned and operated by **Leroy McGuirk** and Cowboy **Bill Watts.** These two really had a genuine "love-hate" relationship, and some of their verbal battles were classics. I learned many new curse words in my early twenties, thanks to these two. Leroy was a former National Amateur Wrestling Champion at Oklahoma A&M, now known as Oklahoma State University, and a former NWA World Junior Heavyweight Champion for many years before a car

Cowboy Bill Watts was a unique individual and knew what he wanted. He was my first boss in the business. The big Cowboy had a brilliant mind for producing episodic, weekly television, but his people skills were often as abrupt as his finishing maneuver, the "Oklahoma Stampede."

accident in Little Rock, Arkansas, took his sight. Leroy usually surrounded himself with old-timers who served no significant purpose but to keep McGurik company, stir controversy, and keep the volatile Cowboy in a hostile mood, which usually did not take too much effort.

Watts was a super heavyweight at 300 pounds, the exact opposite of Leroy's favorite division, the junior heavyweights, and played football for the legendary **Bud Wilkinson** at the University of Oklahoma, the arch rival of in-state foe, Oklahoma State. You get the picture. These two business partners had the business in common but that was about it.

The old **National Wrestling Alliance** was a cooperative organization of wrestling promoters around the world who collectively sanctioned the NWA Champion and how he was selected and his touring schedule. The champion traveled thousands and thousands of miles each year, literally around the world, to defend the championship against the best the local wrestling territories/promotions had to offer. The NWA Champion in those days had to be a talented in-ring performer with the ability to wrestle heroes or villains and make them look good even though the local talent would rarely if ever win the title. The champion also had to be able to take care of himself, just in case some local star got a wild hair and went into business for himself with designs on winning the coveted championship and making a name for himself. The NWA board of directors selected the champion every year at their annual meeting where usually all the promoters would gather, address the championship situation, the state of the business, drink good booze, smoke expensive cigars, and generally b.s. each other.

Prior to the annual meeting in about 1972 or 1973, Cowboy was on the phone in the Tulsa office campaigning for a particular wrestler to be appointed the next NWA Champion. I had been asked to leave the room just prior to this conversation commencing, so I did not know which promoter Watts was speaking with, though I think it was **Bob Geigel,** who promoted for decades out of Kansas City. The conversation went on for about fifteen minutes, and standing in the outer office I could hear the big Cowboy's booming voice get louder and louder.

"ENGELBERT HUMPERDINCK . . . DAMMIT!! ENGELBERT HUMPERDINCK FOR GOD'S SAKES!! WHAT'S THE MATTER WITH YOU??!!

Just then, I heard **Mr. McGuirk** call out my name, and the blind promoter asked me to accompany him to the men's room, which he usually handled alone. It was amazing what this man could do even though he had no sight. I meekly walked into the office and got the look of death from Watts. His face had turned beet red and his veins were bulging from his neck as he listened to the person on the other end of the phone.

Mr. McGuirk and I walked down the hall, and he took care of his business and was washing his hands when I worked up the courage to ask him if he was also endorsing the singer Engelbert Humperdinck to become the NWA Champion? (Which was almost as ridiculous as when **actor David Arquette** became WCW Champion a few years ago.)

"No, kid. We don't want Engelbert Humperdinck to be Champion, we want Jack Brisco to be the next NWA Champion!"

Then I got it. **Jack Brisco,** who would become one of my all-time favorite ring performers and a treasured personal friend, was a former stud amateur at Oklahoma State University and was an undefeated National Champion for the OSU Cowboys. He had pinned every opponent he faced his last year in Stillwater and had gone on to become an amazing pro. And the handsome Native American from Blackwell, Oklahoma, also had an uncanny resemblance to the hot singing star of that era. Cowboy was trying to describe Jack Brisco as a wrestling star with the potential to appeal to female fans as well as males, because of his handsome features. The bombastic Cowboy was passionately trying his best to convince what had to be an old-school promoter that Brisco was the man for the job. I naïvely thought that the new guard was trying to *really* shake things up and make a famous recording star the coveted **NWA Champion.**

THE TOP TEN THINGS WWE LOOKS FOR IN A YOUNG WRESTLER

10 Reliability   **9** Respect for themselves and others

8 Willingness to make sacrifices to achieve their goals

7 Family support

6 Character

5 Verbal skills

4 Intelligence

3 Being a true fan of the business

2 Athleticism

1 Passion for the product

This is Senior Vice President business going on (you can tell because I'm not wearing my black hat) in this casual conversation with Chavo Guerrero.

J.R.'S TOP TEN RETIRED (or close to it) WRESTLERS OF ALL TIME

10 **The Assassins** (Jody Hamilton and Tom Renesto) —Best villain team **I ever saw. They gave me nightmares as a kid!**

9 Ernie Ladd—**Did more for African-American wrestlers than anyone I ever knew. Ernie had consummate crowd psychology. Ernie was a** Grambling football legend **and a standout AFL defensive lineman. I sat for many hours under Ernie's "Learning Tree."**

8 The Funks **(Terry and Dory) and Dusty Rhodes (tie)—All three of these men had West Texas State ties, and all three could put "asses in the seats."**

Oklahoma legends ... and J.R. too. From left to right: Danny Hodge, Gerald Brisco, Cowboy Bill Watts, Jack Brisco.

7 Harley Race—One bad apple that was ahead of his time. This Kansas City native was a warhorse and so believable! A great NWA World Champion and tougher than a three-dollar steak.

6 Killer Karl Kox—Knew exactly how to manipulate an audience. He told great stories very authentically. Tough s.o.b.

5 Dick Murdoch—Captain Red-Neck was as good as anyone ever, when he wanted to be serious. Equally as good as a hero or a villain and could he *talk!* Dickie also loved a cold beer.

4 Junkyard Dog—Most popular African-American star ever. He was a bighearted, charismatic ex-footballer who loved to entertain. We both launched our careers in Mid South Wrestling.

3 Cowboy Bill Watts—Brilliant, bombastic, ex-Oklahoma Sooner football player who gave me my start. Cowboy's "promo" ability was awesome. He was a very athletic 300-pounder who sold tickets wherever he went.

2 The Brisco Brothers (Jack and Gerry)—These Blackwell, Oklahoma, Native American brothers were as good a team as I ever saw, and Jack was as good as any NWA Champion that ever laced up his boots. Gerry has become like a brother to me and works with me at WWE.

1 Danny Hodge—From Perry, Oklahoma, Danny was a two-time Olympian and former NWA World Junior Heavyweight Champion. He was the best in his weight class in the history of the pros *and* amateurs. No one else has ever been like this man!

IT TAKES A LOT OF FUEL TO RUN THIS ENGINE!!

For some reason, many people who worked for **Jim Herd** in WCW did not like the man. As a matter of fact, some downright detested him. But not me. Oh, yes, we had plenty of disagreements, and even a shouting match or two, over philosophical issues as they related to our business. Herd was not a product of the wrestling business, as he came from television. He managed KPLR-TV in St. Louis, he did marketing, he worked for the St. Louis Blues of the NHL and even managed a string of Pizza Huts for some rich guy named George. Herd was a stocky, white-haired man who wore an 18-x-32 shirt. I know this because he used to raise hell that he had to order all of his white oxford cloth shirts and could not buy them off the rack because of his big neck and short arms. Even though Mr. Herd may have been in over his head in his role of managing a wrestling company, I, to this very day, believe he was a good-hearted guy who really wanted the company to succeed. He was brought to Turner by his longtime friend and fellow St. Louis resident **Jack Petrik,** one of Ted's right-hand men, to make the division profitable after Turner bought the company from a financially strapped Jim Crockett Promotions. Herd was an emotional man whose eyes would well up with tears via his anger and his heartfelt emotions, but, damn, he hated anyone to see the latter.

I was once summoned to his office to witness a telephone call he was about to have with an angry fan. It seems as if the fan, along with his wife and kids, were waiting to get autographs from some of the wrestlers in the lobby of a hotel. It was after a show and the wrestlers were in the hotel bar, just off the lobby, enjoying libations and attempting to get better acquainted with some of the females in the establishment. One of the wrestlers apparently had a little too much to drink and unzipped his slacks and exposed himself to the young lady of the hour. The young lady with him may have enjoyed what she saw, but the fellow with the wife and kids who saw it all from the lobby did not.

Bottom line: I get this call from Mr. Herd, in his **"Artie"** (the Rip Torn character) of HBO's *The Larry Sanders Show* voice, yelling, "Get down here, we've got a problem!"

No hello, no back story, no nothing. I left my desk in our twelfth-floor offices in the CNN Center in Atlanta and hustled to the boss's office down the hall without a clue about what awaited me. As I got there, Herd was reaching for the phone, but I still had no idea as to why I was there. I soon found out, as the gruff white-haired man put the angry fan on the speakerphone and then proceeded to talk him out of going public about the incident and not filing charges or mounting a lawsuit. The fan got a bunch of free tickets to WCW events, which is ironic, because we sure as hell weren't selling many in those days, and a large box of free merchandise.

After work that day, Mr. Herd and I went to Bone's Restaurant in Atlanta (a helluva place to eat, by the way) and had a few cocktails and "some red meat," as the former Kentucky Wildcat footballer for the legendary **Bear Bryant** used to say.

It is there that he uttered the words I will never forget, as he had about his third or fourth gin and tonic. He said, "By God, it takes a lot of fuel to run this engine!"

There are plenty of great **"Jim Herd"** stories I will never forget, and I only wish my colleagues who never liked him could have gotten to know him better, and that he had gotten more credit for the job he did in the early days of WCW.

"By God, it takes **a lot** *of fuel to run this engine!"*

HE WAS ONCE ONE OF THE MOST INFLUENTIAL MEN IN WRESTLING . . . AND BY THE WAY, HE'S ALSO GAY

My friend **Jim Barnett** and I have a great deal in common. Now wait a minute, before you jump to conclusions, let me explain. Jim and I obviously have the same first name, we are both natives of Oklahoma, and we both have dedicated our adult lives to the wrestling business. Since the early 1950s and after graduating from the University of Chicago, Jim Barnett has been a key figure in the worldwide development of professional wrestling in a variety of front-office positions and ownership roles in a number of successful wrestling promotions and territories. Jim was involved in the business when the Dumont Network aired wrestling nationally in the early 1950s and was instrumental in the introduction on that network of a young University of Minnesota wrestling and football star, Verne Gagne, among so many others, who went on to become one of the business's most significant individuals. Jim also owned the Georgia territory and as a result became close friends with Ted Turner, the founder of Turner Broadcasting, which aired Georgia Championship Wrestling with **Gordon Solie.** Along the way Jim developed a relationship with Jimmy Carter, who was then governor of Georgia, and went on to become the thirty-ninth president of the United States. Mr. Barnett, or James E.—as many of his friends have called him over the years—was even appointed by President Carter to the National Council for the Arts and attended Carter's inauguration with the Georgian's family and close friends.

James E. also pioneered the wrestling business in Australia in the 1960s and opened a territory there that became one of the most successful in the world at the time. Some of the biggest stars in the business worked there, including the **Briscos,** Killer Kowalski, Killer Karl Kox, Pat Patterson, Spiros Arion, Billy Robinson, and others too numerous to mention. Jim worked in executive roles with WWE and the NWA. He brokered the sale of Jim Crockett Promotions to Ted Turner, which formed WCW. He owned part of the Florida territory at one time. Jim Barnett, without question, was one of the business's most influential men for close to half a century, and he happens to be gay—not that there is anything wrong with that. He is also one of the most interesting characters I have *ever* met or worked with in the wrestling business. Someday I will tell some of the "Jim Barnett" stories I have heard. I witnessed many of them, and he has become one of the most impersonated men ever within our crazy business.

Jim is a cross between Truman Capote and Mr. Magoo, and virtually everyone who has ever met him can offer an impersonation of him. Be that as it may, Jim made it big in a business and at a time when gay men simply were not socially accepted or—oftentimes—respected by their peers, especially in the old-time wrestling business that was dotted with rough, tough, cigar-chomping, macho men in positions of power and ownership. Through all this prejudice and ridicule, however, Jim Barnett steered the course and never allowed the narrow-mindedness of others to force him to leave his chosen profession.

I have had many interesting discussions with Jim over the years, and someday I hope to write about them in more depth because they are simply fascinating. His personal interactions with Rock Hudson, Montgomery Clift, and others in the golden era of Hollywood are amazing. I admire Jim's professional accomplishments. No one I know had to work harder to make it in this business and to be accepted than **James E. Barnett.**

TOP **TEN** REASONS WHY J.R. LOVES THIS BUSINESS

10 Travel—really. **Sometime it's great! Gotta love those frequent flier miles.**

9 **Twenty-four-hour** room service—food **had to make this list in some form!**

8 **Fun—the** opportunity to have fun. **Some we talk about, some we can't.**

7 Friends—the many friends around the world I have made in over two decades in this business.

6 Never a dull moment— every single day often seems like a different adventure.

5 Drama— suspending all disbelief when the true art forms come together in the ring.

4 Athleticism—with over 200 one-night stands a year, wrestlers puts their bodies at risk virtually every moment of every performance.

3 The passion—from the performers and the fans. When all goes right in the ring, it is an unbelievable combination.

2 The talent—the greatest athletic performers on the face of the earth, who rarely get the credit they deserve.

1 The fans—the overall most loyal group of human beings around the globe who often suffer unjust ridicule from insecure, ill-informed critics of our business.

J.R.'S TOP TEN PET PEEVES ABOUT CERTAIN TYPES OF WRESTLERS

10 Con men who think they are getting away with something and outsmarting the system.

9 Talent with poor time-management skills who are always late for work.

8 Always a "steak eater" in catering, but can't perform with bumps and bruises.

7 In the business simply for the money.

6 Playing video games in the locker room when they should be observing their peers in the ring and learning something.

5 Veterans who do not know when to "hang 'em up" and are holding back good young talents.

4 Great body, no heart . . . muscle-heads with a baby-oil fetish.

3 Dressing room lawyers.

2 Liars.

1 "I don't mind doing it personally, but my character says no."

J.R.'s Glossary of Cooking and Grilling Terms

Al dente When pasta is cooked just enough to be firm and chewy—not overcooked. Means "to the tooth" in Italian. My wife told me.

Au gratin Cooking with a topping of bread crumbs and cheese and grilled to a golden brown color in the oven.

Bake To cook food in the oven. The food is cooked slowly with all-around heat, causing the natural moisture to evaporate, building the flavor.

Baste To brush or spoon liquid, drippings, or juices on the meat while cooking to add flavor and moisture.

Batter A mixture of flour, egg, and milk that is used to coat items you are going to fry, like chicken, for example. Or it can be a mixture used to bake a cake. It can also be a verb, like "I'm gonna batter those chicken parts so I can fry 'em up."

Beat To blend a mixture by briskly stirring it with a spoon, fork, wire whisk, or mixer.

Bias-slice To slice food crosswise at a 45-degree angle.

Blackened A popular Cajun-style cooking technique where seasoned foods are cooked over high heat in a superheated heavy iron skillet until charred. Many times the food is coated with crushed peppercorns.

Blanching To dip in boiling water for a short time and then in cold water to remove the outer skin. Used for tomatoes, almonds, etc.

Blend To mix two or more ingredients together to get 'em all combinded together real good.

Boil To cook food in heated water on the stove.

Braise A cooking technique that requires browning the meat in oil in a pan and then cooking slowly in liquid to tenderize the meat.

Bread To coat the food with dry bread crumbs or flour. Sometimes the bread crumbs or flour have seasoning in them. The food is usually dipped in an egg wash first to make the crumbs stick to the food.

Brochette It means "kebob," in French; food grilled on a skewer.

Broil To cook food directly under a high-heat source, like the broiler in your oven.

Brown A quick sautéing in a pan on the stove top, in the oven, or on the grill that is done either at the beginning or at the end of the food preparation to enhance flavor, and make it look *good*!

Brush To use a bristled brush to coat and paint food such as meat or bread with melted butter, sauce, or other liquid before or even while cooking.

Butterfly When you cut food open down the center without cutting all the way through it, and then spread it apart. This can be done with pork chops, steak fillets, or shrimp. It's a good way to cook a thick fillet to medium-well or well-done, if that's what you want.

Caramelizing To brown sugar over a flame, sometimes with liquid added, like water or butter.

Charcoal grate The grate is the rack that holds the charcoal off the bottom of the pit, grill, or cooker.

Charcoal grill A cooking grill that uses charcoal briquettes to cook food.

Chimney starter A metal cylinder-shaped gadget used to start charcoal. It works quickly, so you don't need lighter fluid.

Chop To cut food into small pieces. If using a knife, put a cutting board underneath the food!

Clarify To remove impurities from butter by heating it and then straining or skimming it to make it clear.

Coat To evenly cover food with flour, crumbs, or batter.

Deep-fry To completely submerge the food in hot oil and fry it until crisp.

Dice To cut food into very small even cubes.

Direct grilling Quickly cooking food by placing it on a grill rack directly above the heat. Food is usually cooked uncovered on a charcoal grill, but covered on a gas grill.

Disjoint To cut meat or chicken at the bone joints.

Dredge To coat meat, chicken, or fish with your flour/coating mixture by rolling the food in a pan filled with the flour mixture.

Dress To clean and trim chicken or fruit and vegetable.

Drip pan A metal foil pan placed under food to catch drippings when grilling. You can also make a drip pan from heavy foil.

Drippings Use this for gravies and sauces, or for basting. Drippings are the juices left in the bottom of a pan after the meat is cooked.

Drizzle To pour a liquid such as a sauce, glaze or melted butter in a slow, light manner over food.

Dry smoking A method of cooking foods by placing it on a grill rack indirectly over the heat source with the lid down and vents adjusted to allow the fire to burn and create smoke.

Dust To sprinkle food lightly with spices, sugar, or flour to make a light coating.

Egg wash Mix beaten eggs (yolks, whites, or whole eggs) with either milk or water to coat cookies and other baked goods to give them a shine when baking. Chicken can also be dipped in an egg wash before dredging the chicken in flour before frying.

Entrée In the United States, *entrée* refers to the main dish of a meal.

Filet A piece of fish or meat without bones.

Fillet To remove bones from meat or fish before cooking.

Filter To remove lumps, excess liquid, or particles by passing food through a paper or cheesecloth strainer.

Flambé To ignite a sauce (usually alchohol based) so that it flames up in the pan.

Flare-ups Flames caused by fat dripping onto the hot coals.

Folding A method used for mixing food items. It is done with a careful lifting and dropping motion.

Fricassee A stew in which the meat is cut up, cooked in some butter, and then simmered in liquid until done.

Fritter A sweet deep-fried food.

Fry To cook food in hot oil until there is a crispy brown crust.

Garnish A decorative, but edible, ingredient, such as parsley, carrot sticks, lemon wedges, etc., placed on the plate as a finishing touch.

Gas grill A grill that uses a propane tank or a natural gas line for fuel.

Glaze To form a glossy, flavorful coating on food as it cooks, usually by basting.

Grate To shred a food into fine pieces by rubbing it against a rough surface, like a cheese grater.

Gravy Don't forget the gravy! This is usually made from pan drippings, flour, and water. It all depends on what kind of gravy you're making—brown gravy, cream gravy, whatever. By the way, since living near New York City, I've gotten multicultural. I found out that a lot of Italian families up here in the Northeast call their pasta sauce "gravy." I just thought I'd add that because I bet no one in the South ever heard this. So to all cultures in America, some kind of "gravy" is crucial to the meal.

Grease To coat a pan or skillet with a thin layer of oil or shortening.

Grid The metal rods that hold the food on a grill; also called a grill grate.

Grill To cook food over fire or coals, usually done outdoors.

Grill basket A hinged wire basket that's used to hold fish, scallops, or vegetables for grilling.

Grind To cut a food into small pieces using some kind of a gadget.

Indirect grilling Method of cooking food slowly, off to one side of the heat, usually over a drip pan in a covered grill.

Kebobs Pieces of meat, poultry, seafood, and/or vegetables stuck on a skewer and grilled over the fire.

Kettle grill A round charcoal grill with a heavy cover. It usually stands on three legs and can be used for either direct or indirect grilling. These have been around forever.

Knead To work dough with the heels of your hands, folding it back and forth, until it becomes well mixed and stretchy.

Loin A cut of meat that comes from the back of the animal.

Marble To swirl one food into another in a bowl, usually something liquid.

Marbled Meat that is marbled has fat running through it in various quantities.

Marinate To soak food in a flavorful liquid and blend of seasonings before it is cooked. Marinades add flavor to foods and tenderize certain cuts of meat.

Mash To beat or press food, like potatoes, to remove lumps and make a smooth mixture.

Medallion A small round or oval-shaped piece of meat.

Medium done For this doneness, the center of the meat should have a slight pink to red color. If using a thermometer, medium done is 160° F.

Medium-rare done For this doneness, the center of the meat should have a bright red color. If using a thermometer, medium-rare is 145° F.

Medium-well done The center of the meat should have very little pink color. If using a thermometer, medium-well temperature is 170° F.

Meringue Egg whites beaten until they are stiff and then sweetened to be used as a pie topping.

Mince To chop food into small irregular pieces.

Mix To beat or stir two or more foods together until they are thoroughly blended together.

Moisten Adding small amounts of liquid to ingredients to dampen but not soak them.

Pan broil To cook food in a skillet without adding fat and removing any fat as it accumulates.

Pan fry To cook in a hot pan on top of the stove with a small amount of oil, butter, or other fat, turning the food over until done.

Parboil To partly cook food in a boiling liquid.

Pesto A sauce usually made of fresh basil, garlic, olive oil, pine nuts, and cheese. The uncooked ingredients are finely chopped and mixed with pasta. Generally, pesto refers to any uncooked sauce made of finely chopped herbs and/or nuts.

Poach To simmer food in liquid.

Purée To mash or sieve food into a thick liquid.

Reconstitute To take a dried food and bring it back to its original state by adding liquid.

Reduce To cook liquids down so that some of the water evaporates and causes the liquid to thicken.

Render To melt fat down to make drippings.

Roast To cook meat without a cover in the oven.

Rotisserie The spit, or long metal skewer, that holds and rotates the food over the grill.

Roux A cooked paste usually made from flour, butter, spices, and other "secret ingredients" used to thicken sauces or make gumbo.

Rub A blend of seasonings, many times a family secret, that is rubbed onto the food's surface before grilling.

Sauce As in "J.R.'s BBQ Sauce," for example. There's all kinds of sauces out there, so take your pick, but be sure to use a good one!

Sauté A method of brisk cooking by tossing the food in a pan in cooking oil and by moving the pan very quickly backward and forward over a high flame.

Score Making a number of shallow, often diagonal, cuts across the meat's surface with a sharp knife, usually to help tenderize it. This is also useful when marinating, as it helps the liquid to absorb into the meat better.

Sear Seal in the juices by cooking meat quickly over very high heat.

Season To enhance the flavor of food by adding salt and pepper and a variety of other herbs and spices. "Season" also refers to treating a cast-iron pan with a coating of cooking oil and baking it for 1 hour at 350° F to make the pan nonstick.

Set To let food "stabilize" and become solid, or "ready," for example, after taking food off the heat source.

Shred To cut or tear food into long narrow strips.

Sift To remove large lumps from a dry ingredient, such as flour or sugar, by passing it through a fine mesh, like a strainer. This process also adds air, making them lighter.

Simmer Cooking food in liquid at low temperature so that small bubbles begin to form.

Skewer A long wooden or metal needle used to thread small pieces of meat or vegetable for grilling.

Skim To remove the top layer of fat from stock, soup, sauces, or other liquids, like milk.

Smoker box A small, perforated steel or iron container placed on a gas grill's rocks or briquettes, to hold wet wood chips to provide smoke and extra flavor.

Steam To cook food in a covered pan over boiling water, letting the steam cook the food.

Steep To soak dry ingredients in liquid until the flavor is absorbed into the liquid.

Stewing To brown small pieces of meat, chicken, or fish and then simmer them with vegetables in enough liquid to cover them, usually in a pot with a lid on the stove or with a slow cooker.

Stir-fry To fast fry small pieces of meat and vegetables over high heat with continuous and rapid stirring in a frying pan or a Chinese wok.

Thin To reduce the thickness of something, usually a liquid, with the addition of more liquid.

Toss To combine ingredients thoroughly by mixing in a bowl with salad spoons or two large spoons.

Truss To use string, pins, or skewers to hold meat or poultry together while cooking to maintain its shape.

Vents Holes in a grill or firebox that open and close. Air circulates through, increasing the heat of the fire when the vents are open.

Vinaigrette A sauce or dressing made with vinegar, oil, and seasonings.

Whip To mix air into cream or egg whites, for example, by beating them until light and fluffy.

Wood chips or wood pellets Natural wood or hardwood materials added to a fire to impart smoky flavor to food as it cooks. Soak these for an hour first to make 'em really smoke good and not catch on fire.

Index

J.R.'s BBQ Sauce and J.R.'s Hot Sauce can be purchased at wwe.com. Click on Shopzone.

Head Country BBQ Seasoning can be obtained by calling 888-762-1227 or visiting www.headcountry.com.